Anonymous

Report of the House Committee on Investigation of the Affairs of

the State Prison South

Anonymous

Report of the House Committee on Investigation of the Affairs of the State Prison South

ISBN/EAN: 9783744752077

Printed in Europe, USA, Canada, Australia, Japan

Cover: Foto ©Suzi / pixelio.de

More available books at **www.hansebooks.com**

COMMITTEE REPORT.

Your Committee on the Affairs of the State Prison South, pursuant to instructions, have made an investigation of the management and condition of said institution, and beg leave to submit the following report:

Your Committee secured the services of Mr. J. W. Coons, an expert accountant, who, having been first duly sworn, in connection with your Committee, proceeded to examine the financial management and condition of said Prison. We find that the books are kept, and have been for years, in a manner utterly unlike those of an ordinary business establishment. There is no general ledger, journal or blotter showing the receipts and disbursements. There is no system whatever in the manner of book-keeping. It does not even show in any one account the money received from the State Treasury for the maintenance of said institution; nor are separate accounts kept with the contractors of the convict labor, from which the Prison derives its earnings, and in order to ascertain the condition of these accounts, it becomes necessary to go back to previous months on a book, named "Time Book," and add the several amounts there charged, and in many instances marked "partly paid."

A. J. Howard, Warden, under oath, testified as follows:

"As Warden of the Southern State Prison of Indiana, I am willing to and do admit that the books of the Southern State Prison show a greater amount due the State, greater than I can now account for, and more than I am able or willing to pay, believing as I do that the books are incorrect, and that I am entitled to credits which the books do not show."

We find that the books were under the control of Mr. A. J. Howard, Warden, and the evidence discloses the fact that Mr. M. I. Huette, Clerk of the Prison, was prohibited from making entries on the cash book, save as permitted and directed to do so by the Warden in person. It is also in evidence that entries in said cash book were made of bills as paid, when in fact they were not paid, such entries being made for exhibit to the Directors, and that the Cleik, in order to know the true financial status of the Institution, kept a private ledger for himself.

The short time your Committee was able to give to the investigation of the books and accounts prevented it from making a thorough examination of them. From our examination, we find the following :

RECEIPTS.

From Treasurer of State on account of settlement for the month of November, 1886, not accounted for	$3,222 22	
Sundry receipts for November	2,745 27	
Sundry receipts for December	12,070 16	
Sundry receipts for January, 1887	2,704 27	
Sundry receipts fractional month February (10th included)	2,739 37	
Cash in visitors' fund	1,367 92	
Cash in convicts' savings fund	3,645 21	
Cash in *brick-yard fund	6,000 00	
Cash in confiscation fund	45 60	
†Pension money of Convict Sanders	2,200 00	
		$36,740 02

DISBURSEMENTS.

Sundry accounts as per cash book, November	$5,967 49	
Sundry accounts as per cash book, December	6,370 26	
Sundry accounts January, and up to February 16, 1887	3,887 31	
Excess payments of vouchers during January	479 39	
Balance to be accounted for	20,035 57	
		$36,740 02

No record is kept to show the bills payable. The following accounts are found filed in the office of the Prison, and are admitted to be correct by A. J. Howard, Warden:

M. V. McCann, coal	$1,642 45
Payne & Ragsdale, provisions	786 25
E. C. Eaken & Co., groceries	1,474 81
Lewman Bros., drugs and hardware	673 82
Jeff. Gas Co., gas	324 00
Perin & Gaff, merchandise.	147 93
Sundry newspapers, advertising	185 82
Geo. Willacy, queensware	30 80
O. F. Zimmerman (?)	40 25
Myer & Bros., lumber	45 12
Chas. Nagle, ice	25 00
J. H. Zinsmeister & Bros., grocery	34 05
L. P. Byland, teamster	151 50
E. J. Howard, lumber	156 42
Ohrens & Ott, pumps, etc	74 30
Geo. F. Frank, saddlery.	34 00
Geo. Hulzbog, carriagemaker	33 70
J. H. Hodapp, produce	178 65
P. Treacy, grocery	3 44
Oglesby & Dustin, produce	65 50
B. T. Babbitt, soap	38 99
Ohio Valley Telegraph Co., telegrams	8 90
G. W. Baxter, Deputy Warden	6 80
A. M. Bloom, meat	1,134 00
Salaries of guards and employes, November	2,229 82
Salaries of guards and employes, December	2,512 23
Salaries of guards and employes, January	2,528 47
Seymour Woolen Factory, merchandise	1,025 33
Total	$15,592 35

This sum of $15,592.35 does not include the accounts payable for the month of February, 1887, nor does it include accounts not yet presented for payment, if any, for previous months, for the reason that no records are kept showing such transactions, and for the further reason that the Warden and Clerk were unable to give such information.

The "Private Ledger," kept aside from the books of the prison by M. I. Huette, the Clerk (no other books showing such information), shows that there is due the State of Indiana from the following named contractors, on account of convict labor, long since due, the following sums, to-wit:

Perin & Gaff Manufacturing Co............................... $225 04
Thomas Gaff.. 5,874 43
Frank L. Perin................................. .... 3,002 36
R. M. Dennis.. 393 80
                                                            ———————
Total...$9,495 63

The bank and check-book of the Warden used in the transaction of his official business would have been of great value in making this examination, and would, perhaps, have shown transactions impossible to arrive at in any other way; but as he, the said Warden, refused to comply with the demand of your Committee to produce said books, the investigation was made without same.

The brick-yard fund heretofore mentioned in this report was not examined by us for the reason that the Warden failed to produce the vouchers claimed to have been paid out of this fund. Warden Howard testified that the total amount of this account was between $14,000 and $15,000, but claimed the balance now due the State to be $2,700. The estimated charge of $6,000 against him, as given in this report, is based upon testimony before the Committee.

The convicts' savings account is the only ledger account kept in the prison. Upon examination of this book we find that many convicts, now and heretofore confined in the prison, are and have been subscribers to the Jeffersonville Evening Times, a daily newspaper published in Jeffersonville, and owned by Mr. A. J. Howard, Warden, for which paper the convict is charged $4.20 per annum, or 35 cents per month. It is in evidence that the librarian, a convict named Martin, solicited subscriptions for this paper, and more copies of it entered the prison than any other paper.

We further find that the guards and employes of the prison have not received their monthly wages for November, December and January, amounting to $7,270.52, and that the Warden, upon settlement with the Auditor of State, for the month of November, drew from the State Treasury the amount of wages of said guards and employes for said month of November, amounting to the sum of $2,229.82, which amount is included in the sum of $3,222.22, heretofore charged against said Warden, for the reason that the same had not been accounted for on the books of the prison.

We further find that it has been customary for bills rendered to remain unpaid for a considerable length of time, ranging from four to fifteen months. Among such bills, we find one from the Seymour Woolen Factory, $2,645, made out in November, 1885, and paid on February 16, 1887. We also find in the office of the Warden a number of, unopened letters addressed to A. J. Howard, Warden. Many of these letters were received five and six months ago, and were found to relate to the business transactions of the prison.

We also find that the Warden has been in the habit of borrowing money from his subordinate officers for the purpose of paying the gate money of discharged convicts, and that said money is still owing.

The item of $2,200, with which said Howard is charged in this report, is explained as follows: Isaac W. Sanders, a lifetime convict, during the month of August, 1886, received arrearages of pensions to the amount of $2,727.75, granted on account of wounds received during the late war. Said Howard, as Warden, deposited the amount, less $427.75 used by said Sanders, in the Citizens' National Bank, Jeffersonville, to the credit of said Sanders. For this balance of $2,200 a certificate of deposit was issued to Sanders. At the urgent request of said Warden Howard, said Sanders indorsed said certificate of deposit in favor of said Warden. Sanders in evidence stated that he would not have done so under any other circumstances, and we find it was done under duress. The money obtained thereon your committee believe to have been part of the cash exhibited to the Senate Investigating Committee as part of the cash account of said prison. After your Committee was in possession of these facts, and before your Committee had left the prison, Mr. A. J. Howard, after he had resigned his office as Warden, presented through the clerk, Mr. Huette, said amount of $2,200 to the chairman of your Committee, whereupon same was paid over to the Acting Warden, Mr. Baxter, who deposited the same to the credit of said Sanders.

There is no way of determining, from the appearance of the books, how many tickets of admission have been sold to visitors to the prison at the entrance charge of 25 cents each, as the tickets were kept in an open box in the office, and were indiscriminately sold by persons in and about the office. No correct account was ever kept of the sales of such tickets, and but a small percentage of the amount accruing therefrom was ever accounted for. We find from the evidence that the average attendance daily was not less than eight paying persons, aggregating an amount of over $700 per annum. The proceeds of this fund was supposed to be applied to the purchase of books for the prison library. Chaplain Cain, in giving evidence, stated that during his tenure of office, three years and three months, he bought but $225 worth of books. The item of $1,367.92, charged as Visitors' Fund, is the accumulated amount of years, found on the books.

We find that, in order to make a "good showing" in his annual reports, the said Warden has not complied with the law regulating the payments of "Earnings and Receipts" into the State Treasury. He has been in the habit of making use of the appropriations for the new fiscal year for debts accrued during the previous years, and consequently his accounts do not agree with the accounts kept in the office of the Auditor of State. (See title-page of Report of State Prison South, signed "James H. Rice, Auditor of State.")

We find that for years the Warden and Deputy Warden have appropriated to their own use flour belonging to the prison, and garden truck and vegetables, cultivated by convict labor from ground belonging to the State, without any account being made therefor or record kept thereof. It is also in evidence that raw material belonging to the State and convict labor have been otherwise appropriated for private use and the State charged for same.

It is impossible at this time, on account of the irregular manner of book-keeping and on account of the refusal of said Warden to produce his bank and check books, and other books, papers and vouchers, to arrive at the true financial condition of the prison, but from the partial examination we were enabled to make, and from information from a reliable source as to outstanding accounts, and moneys received and not accounted for, and peculations, your committee is of the opinion that there is a deficit amounting to $75,000. This deficiency does not embrace Mr. A. J. Howard's entire term of office as Warden, as such an examination would require the services of two expert accountants for several weeks, but it is evident that the deficit for his twelve years of service would aggregate a much larger sum, consisting of moneys received and unaccounted for, false entries and omissions.

We find that the said A. J. Howard did not file a new bond upon his re-election to the office of Warden two years ago, and upon his resignation it appeared that there were no State moneys on hand, and the Deputy Warden was obliged to advance from his private funds the gate money for a pardoned convict.

Your Committee would recommend that the facts herein recited be communicated to the Attorney-General for his action in the premises; that some method be adopted by the House to ascertain the exact amount of defalcation, and that the new Warden be required to strike a balance, and open and keep the accounts systematically, in a full set of books to be furnished for the use of said Prison.

We find that the Directors then in office are censurable in not requiring the execution of a new bond at the re-election of Warden Howard; that the present Directors of said Prison, with the exception of Mr. Horn, do not make the periodical visits enjoined by law; that they are directly culpable for the loose and irregular manner of book-keeping; that at their meetings no attempt was made to inquire into the Warden's accounts further than to audit bills the payment of which they never investigated, and at times with the knowledge that the same were not paid; that, in general, instead of supervising and acting as a check upon the actions of the Warden, they permitted him to pursue his own course in the management and direction of said Prison, thus showing gross, if not willful, neglect of duty. Your Committee would therefor recommend that the immediate resignation of the present incumbents be requested.

In this connection, we would say that there was evidence upon the fact that money influences, by candidates, are brought to bear upon the election of Warden, and there is testimony to the effect that in the re-election of Mr. A. J. Howard, two years ago, such influences were used, but from the incomplete ·

investigation we were enabled to make, your Committee do not feel warranted in so finding. There is also testimony that contractors pay a premium to officials for the contract, and evidence was offered that the secretary of the company, who sold their contract to the Jeffersonville Boot and Shoe Company, told the superintendent of the latter company that they paid $4,500 for said contract, but said secretary, being in another State, was not accessible to your Committee, and the investigation in this respect could not be pursued further. We do not find any collusion between contractors and the officials or convicts in reference to securing labor without benefit to the State, but are not prepared to say, with the loose system prevailing, that such could not be had.

We find that ex-Deputy Warden Craig, Clerk Huette and Steward Allen are officers of the prison who have long been cognizant of the corrupt practices; that ex-Deputy Warden Craig and Steward Allen were instrumental in covering up the defalcation existing at the time of the legislative investigation two years ago, and that Deputy Warden Baxter and Steward Allen assisted in procuring the private money exhibited to the Senate Investigating Committee of this General Assembly as State funds; and that these officers are deserving of severe censure for not presenting their full knowledge of the corruption to the proper authorities.

We find that the clerk, in addition to his salary, was allowed the privilege of selling soap, underclothing and other articles to the convicts, the proceeds from which amount to about $300 per year. The Steward has, as his perquisites, the bones and empty barrels, making an an item of about $200 per year. This practice we consider obnoxious, to say the least, and we would recommend that these proceeds accrue to the State.

We find that no advertisements for bids on supplies were ever made and contracts let according to law; that provisions were bought in small quantities, and that the coal was furnished monthly by one of the bondsmen of the Warden. The meat, supplied by a Louisville butcher, consists of the quarters and shanks, the choice portions going to other parties.

The meal and hominy are manufactured at the prison. We find that about two-thids of the corn becomes offal, amounting to two or three barrels per day of very rich feed for stock. We find no returns have been made to the State of proceeds derived from such offal.

We find that the large amount of slops and refuse from the table have been wasted or fed to the Warden's hogs.

We would recommend that bids for supplies be solicited by advertisement, and that the lowest bidder be awarded the contract; that the supplies be bought in large quantities for long periods, to be furnished as needed; that a record of the prices paid be kept at both the Northern and Southern State Prisons, for comparison; that the offal and slops be advertised for sale and sold to the highest bidder, and if they can not be disposed of, that the State buy sufficient stock and hogs, if advisable, to be supported therewith; and that all proceeds of whatever nature accruing from State property be applied to the benefit of the State.

From the evidence, we conclude that the quality of food furnished has been decidedly better within the last three or four years. Prior to that time, the Warden supplied the meat for a number of years from a pork-house owned by himself and brother, and it was a frequent occurrence to find the meat rotten and full of maggots. We find the bacon, potatoes and hominy furnished the convicts are in the main of fair quality. The beans used for making soup are musty and partly rotten. The corn bread is of poor quality, the meal not being bolted beyond having the husk taken out.

The outer clothing of convicts is sufficient, but there is much complaint that they are compelled to buy their underclothing from the Clerk at extravagant prices, and are not allowed to receive it from their friends. On this point there is conflict of testimony, but we would recommend that they be allowed to receive such garments, and by stamping the same a disguise in case of an escape can be prevented.

We find that the greater portion of the cells are foul and damp; the straw ticks contain little straw, and are filthy and swarming with bugs; the sheets are said to be changed every two weeks, and many of them we find are not changed that often. Some cells have no pillows, and what pillows there are have but little straw. The care of the cell seems to be left very much to the occupant. We find no regular system of washing, although there are many idle and unemployed prisoners who might be engaged in washing bed clothing. There is no particular system of bathing, and many of the convicts are afflicted with loathsome diseases. Only two candles per week are allowed to each cell. These are consumed in one or two nights, and the convicts thus spend the greater part of the week in idleness and darkness, other than the general lighting of the cell-house. The cell-houses are heated by stoves. The heat they afford can hardly penetrate the cells, and there is much suffering during inclement weather.

We find the library to contain about 2,500 books of a character in general unsuited to the readers. Prisoners are allowed a book every two weeks, and must make a choice from ten to twenty books thrown in a box. There is no attempt to catalogue them and permit a selection, which, we suggest, can be readily done. The Librarian, Martin, a life-time convict, has been in charge of this department for a considerable time, and a change would probably prove a benefit.

The chapel is an unplastered room, uninviting in appearance, cold and cheerless in the winter. During the hot months, owing to the tin roof, there is a prostration by the heat. Services of one hour's duration are held on Sunday. There is and has been no Sunday-school for a long time, and no satisfactory reason is given for its abandonment. The present Chaplain, elected last September, has organized a small school for illiterate convicts and evinces a disposition to do his duty.

We find that the former Chaplain, L. F. Cain, prostituted his official position by making it the means of securing the confidence of convicts and obtaining from them money for the alleged purpose of securing pardons for them, and that a number of the books bought through him for the library were medical works, in the study of which the said Chaplain was then individually interested.

We find in the hospital about fifteen patients who appear satisfied with their surroundings. To general appearance all is kept clean, but on closer inspection we find the walls are full of cock-roaches and the bed clothing shows lack of sufficient washing. Opportunity is given the sick to see the physician twice a day, but we believe the number of sick treated outside in proportion to those treated inside of the hospital to be over-large, indicating a disposition to work the sick. We find the alarming fact that many prisoners who prefer to work are afflicted with loathsome diseases, and no sanitary provision appears to be made in this regard, for which the physician or Directors must be held censurable.

Cruel and inhuman punishment has characterized the administration of Warden A. J. Howard, and there is reason to believe crimes have been committed under the apparent sanction of law. Your Committee made a partial investigation of three very questionable deaths, and from the evidence we are led to believe that:

In 1875 or 1876, one Goddard, a convict, was punished and killed and his body burnt in the furnace. The remains of what was supposed to be a human being were found by the firemen, whose testimony we were unable to secure. They were also seen by a convict, now confined, and his testimony implicates David M. Allen, the present Steward; Mr. Kennedy, a guard now at the Prison, and Mr. Jack Hilliard, then a guard and at present residing in Jeffersonville.

We find that in February, 1881, one O'Neil, a convict, while sick, was unable to perform his task, and without the knowledge of the Prison Physician, Dr. Sherrod, was punished by imprisonment in the cage, by being handcuffed to the door a number of days. When released, he sought out the Doctor, and begged piteously not to be sent back to the cage and for change of work. Dr. Sherrod was indignant, and Mr. Jack Hilliard, a guard, undertook to carry out his wishes. Instead of doing so, O'Neil was again taken back to the cage, remained handcuffed all night, and in the morning was found dead. Before the Coroner arrived, Dr. Jesse McClure, Hospital Steward, under Dr. Sherrod, and two friends, made a post-mortem examination, and stated to the House Investigating Committee, then present, that the death resulted from congestion of the lungs or heart, it is not definite which. In this examination, Dr. Sherrod was ignored, and his orders that the body be not touched until the Coroner arrived, disobeyed. The Coroner, Jacob Ross, made no investigation beyond lifting the sheet, and noticing that such had already been done without authority. In the post-mortem, the heart, lungs and liver were taken out. These, Dr. Sherrod afterward examined and pronounced healthy. Dr. Jesse McClure, on pretense of looking for ulcers, ordered them to be cut to pieces by a hospital nurse, the witness, and in the course of this, made remarks upon their healthy appearance. We believe there was foul play here.

We find that about the same period one Mungo, a colored convict, charged with stealing a file, was catted on the bare back, while on his hands and knees, by John Craig, then Deputy Warden, and a robust man. The evidence is conflicting as to the number of strokes, as counted by convicts, but all agree in putting the number above fifty. Mungo died from the effects of this castigation in great agony.

We believe the evidence adduced warrants immediate action by the Prosecuting Attorney of Clark County. The persons implicated and those cognizant of the facts are mentioned, and a prosecution should at once be instituted to punish the guilty and remove from the innocent the stain of suspicion.

We are gratified to say that no catting has been done for the last three or four years. To whom this should be credited, we are unable to say. The punishment has been much mitigated, but is yet severe. We find the punishment usually inflicted is confinement—sometimes as long as thirty days—in a filthy and dark cell, commonly called the "Cage," fifty feet from the nearest means of warmth, and full of vermin. Here men are handcuffed to the door during the day, fed upon half rations of corn-bread and water, and at night sleep on the stone floor or on lumber brought for that purpose, without bedding or coats. Convicts have been known to have their feet frozen from exposure in this cell.

Another mode of punishment is by solitary confinement:

J. W. Minor, convict, testified that he had been placed in solitary confinement, with the light entirely shut out, for 8 months, because unable to perform his task. Shields, a guard, found Minor in loathsome condition, and with difficulty obtained permission to have him removed and attended by physician. During the whole of this time, Minor was never visited by the Chaplain.

Other modes of punishment are depriving the men of their allowance of tobacco, of their good time, forbidding their writing to or seeing friends, and all these methods of punishment are sometimes inflicted for one offense.

Your Committee find it difficult not to speak with feeling, of still another punishment, and that most dreaded, imprisonment in the "Crazy House," so called because crazy convicts have been confined there, and sane men have almost been crazed by the confinement. It is a small row of cells, filthy and foul.

Charles David, convict, stated in the presence of guard, without denial from the latter, that he had been imprisoned continuously six months in the Crazy House, and fought the rats for his life. These rats come through a small slot 2x8 inches, which is the only means of ventilation and light. He stated he was for four days at a time without water, and drank his own urine.

Wm. Hamlin, a life convict, is now the only prisoner confined in the Crazy House. He is 70 years old; has been in the Prison for 27 years, and for the last 14 years has been insane. The guard stated that he took him out to the light and walked him about every day or so.

This inhuman treatment merits the most severe condemnation, and we recommend the immediate enactment of a law requiring the Governor to take cognizance of the cases of insane prisoners.

We do not find the punishment compatible with the gravity of the offense.

Delaney Lowry left his work for a moment; he was shoveling into a wagon in the prison yard, and went to the engine-room to warm. Confined in his cell since November 8, 1886. The cell is not whitewashed nor ventilated, and is foul and damp. He is much emaciated and suffering from disease, and without medical treatment.

Convict George Whitted, locked up for two days for having 20 cents in his pocket, given him by stranger; deprived of eight days' good time and of his tobacco, put on half rations; first offense.

Geo. Dowell, for talking, put in cage for twenty-five days.

George Frison, put in cage four days for wearing two pairs of pants, when the guard knew he did not have them on.

James Roper, life convict, in cage for three days, because he walked out of line.

Edward G. Lindsey, eight to sixteen days in cage for taking piece of corn bread from another's plate; also deprived of eight days' good time and tobacco.

We do not find the rules for the government and discipline of the prison printed and posted in the cells, as required by law, and the punishment seems to be left very much to the discretion of the guards. Convicts say, when reported and taken before Warden Howard, they are met with a volume of abuse, and the order is given the guard: "Take the — — — — and give him h—l."

We would also say that it is in evidence that whisky was furnished by guards to convicts for money.

Concerning the task work, your Committee find there is much complaint as to overtasking in the foundry, where 40 to 90 molds is a day's labor. We understand 30 molds is usually considered a good day's labor by free men.

In the saddle-tree department, the task is 12 trees a day from raw material, and the punishment for failure is not less than eight days in the cage, and the loss of good time and tobacco. We would call attention to the fact that contractors only pay for the labor they actually receive.

In the kitchen department the men complain of having to work daily two hours extra, and all day Sunday. They go on at 4 a. m. and off at 5:30 p. m.

The crippled men have the same task as the sound.

Your Committee find the buildings, with the exception of the new cell-house and chapel, in a generally dilapidated condition, an unsafe and decayed wooden fence serving as a wall around the late addition to the Prison, and bad sewerage. But we would not recommend any further outlay for improvements than would suffice to build a stockade wall in place of the said wooden fence, believing that the location of said prison is not conducive to the health and comfort of the prisoners, nor to the best interests of the State. An almost thorough renovation is necessary, and we are of the opinion that in a few years the people will demand a removal to a location where nearness to stone-quarries will admit of the erection of suitable buildings, with less cost and better results, than if the same amount were now expended upon improvements.

At the request of Hon. C. L. Jewett, who is trying to secure a pardon for Arthur Brooks, convict from Wayne County, this convict was examined by us. Some misapprehension having arisen as to Mr. Jewett's connection with this matter, the committee desire to say that it is entirely proper and honorable.

Your Committee feel that the investigation they were able to make is not as searching as more time would permit. We have attempted in this report to calmly review the evidence.

All of which is respectfully submitted.

LEE W. SINCLAIR,   GEORGE W. HOBSON,
J. B. PATTEN,   JOHN D. ALEXANDER,
WILLIAM R. PLEAK,   CHARLES W. CRUSON,
F. J. S. ROBINSON,   JOB OSBORN,
2—PRISON.   WM. H. WHITWORTH.

PRISON SOUTH.

The following is the transcript of the testimony taken before the Committee by the stenographer:

AT PRISON, DIRECTORS' ROOM, }
THURSDAY, February 17, 1887. }

Mr. A. J. Howard, having been shown the authority of the Commission, was duly sworn, and testified as follows:

Q. By Mr. Sinclair: I would like to see your bond, if you please.

A. My bond is in Indianapolis.

Q. What is the date of it?

A. I don't remember the date.

Q. By Mr. Alexander: Who are your bondsmen?

A. As I recollect, Jonas G. Howard, Jonas W. Howard, George F. Howard and M. V. McCann; all live in Clark County.

Q. How long have you been Warden?

A. Eleven years and over.

Q. Do you know how many bonds you have executed to the State?

A. I do not, sir.

Q. Do you remember having executed more than one.

A. Yes, sir, I executed two certainly, probably three.

Q. When you were re-elected Warden two years ago, do you remember of having then executed another bond?

A. Well, I don't know whether I executed another bond or not; the old bond was straight. I don't care to have that part of it put down. It was passed by at that time—was overlooked. I don't know that I ever did file a new bond; the old bond was presumed to be good. There was nothing said of it at that time.

Q. How long after that did you have a conversation with the Directors about it?

A. Sometime after they spoke about it. It was a matter of omission on my part; the gentleman I expected to go on my bond—Jonas Howard—was away at the time.

Q. Has there ever been anything said about it at any of the last meetings of the Directors.

A. No, sir, not recently.

Q. When was your last report made?

A. In December, for fiscal year ending October 31, 1886.

Q. I understand you then not to have filed a bond the last time you were re-elected?

A. My recollection is that I have not yet filed a new bond. The business is standing on the old bond.

Q. By Mr. Patten: You filed a bond in 1882 or 1883 after you was elected?

A. Yes, sir; in 1881.

Q. By Mr. Alexander: Have you made any contracts with any parties since October 31, 1886, for work about the prison—hired out any convicts?

A. No, sir; not since that time. Well, yes, one contract, but I believe it is referred to in my report, page 12. "With R. M. Dennis, manufacturer of saddle-trees, to expire December 31, 1891, thirty convicts, with privilege of fifty."

Q. What was the gross amount paid?

A. Fifty-five cents per day per man.

Q. How much have you received in gross since that report on this contract?

A. I have received on that contract in November, December, January and down to date, $881.89.

Q. What other moneys have you received since that time on any account in the aggregate?

A. For November... $2,745 27
For December (which includes State item deficit, $2,665.33)... 12,070 16
For January... 2,704 27
To February 10...........:............................. 2,739 37
                                                      _____
        Total..$20,259 07

Q. What is the amount credited to convicts' savings?

A. To February 10, $3,645.21.

Q. Give your expenditures since October 31?

A. For November, $5,967.49; for December, $6,370.26.

January and February accounts are not made up yet, but the disbursements since December 31, 1886, to date, are as follows:

Boot and Shoe Co...	$378	00
Geo. F. Howard.............................	100	00
C. Kiselman..	33	00
S. Taylor...	30	69
Zier & Co...	10	50
W. E. Dalton...	50	00
Discharged convicts, January.......................	330	00
Petty cash, January.............................	68	87
Jeffersonville Boot and Shoe Co....................	16	69
S. Jamison, salary.............................	60	00
C. A. Ballou, salary.............................	50	00
Petty cash, February.............................	25	31
Discharged convicts.............................	120	00
Seymour Woolen Factory Co....................	2,614	25
Total...	$3,887	31

Q. By Mr. Patten: This last item of $2,614.25, when did you pay that?

A. Yesterday.

Q. To whom did you pay that?

A. To Mr. Sneck, of Seymour.

Further examination of Mr. A. J. Howard, February 18:

Q. By Mr. Alexander: What is the amount of the brick-yard fund?

A. That brick-yard fund, exclusive of some credits that I claim on final settlement, would amount to a balance of about $2,700 due the State.

Q. Where are the papers in connection with that?

A. I have the vouchers. I made a collection of $6,000 from the Southwestern Car Company, and we had no fund to run the brick-yard account, and I turned it into it. We were making these brick buildings.

Q. That was when they went into bankruptcy. It was the dividend you received from Colonel Merryweather?

A. Yes, sir. I received $6,000. I want to state to you

that I want to go over that brick-yard account and arrange things before I submit them. There are some things that I am entitled to credit. I tried to get at it, but I was telegraphed to come to Indianapolis on account of the Senate Committee report.

Q. Where are the papers in connection therewith?

A. There are some bills that were not reduced to vouchers. I had these papers and had some charges ever since I was paying the expenses out of that in building this cell-house. We furnished the brick for the cell-house out of the brick-yard account. The whole account amounts to about $14,000; with the credits, brings it down to about $2,700.

Q. I would like to look at those papers?

A. I will show them to you this afternoon. I will hunt them up.

Q. By Mr. Patten: State if the brick was not made by convict labor:

A. Except the Superintendent, yes, sir. We had the guards in the yard. We had to buy the wood and hire some free labor occasionally to help us in burning the brick. Had to work a night force.

Q. How many brick were made?

A. I don't know, sir; I don't remember.

Q. How much wood did you burn?

A. I don't remember.

Q. Did you keep an account between yourself and the State in reference to that matter?

A. We kept a brick yard account on side books.

Q. Where are those side books now?

A. I can find them, I guess. I had those papers here at my house to see what they were, when I got a dispatch to come to Indianapolis. I sold some brick that went to swell that amount up. Sold it to J., M. & I. R. R., my recollection is, to build that depot at Columbus.

Q. Do you remember how much you got for that?

A. No, sir, I don't. I remember they run their cars down here on the side track, and we loaded them on the cars.

Q. Captain, we would like you to give us a statement of how much outstanding indebtedness there is against the Prison?

A. I shall have to see the Clerk about that.

Q. Here is a statement of bills payable, made by the Clerk, amounting to $14,000; are there any other? Don't you owe the Seymour Woolen Factory some more money? [Statement attached marked Exhibit B.]

A. I paid them, three or four days ago, $2,600 or so, which left a balance of $371.90.

Q. [Showing bills in blank of Seymour Woolen Factory.] Are these accounted for?

A. No. When I was settling with Mr. Sneck, when I was figuring up that account, I did not know how to extend these items.

Q. Captain, there is a letter in December, from the Seymour Woolen Factory. Here is one in February. Here is another dated December 24. [Handing unopened letters.]

A. These contain the items extended. That amounts to $1,025.33 since October 31. There is nothing paid on that. That is the only item that I know of that is not included in Captain Huette's statement.

Q. State how much money you hold, as Warden, as a pension fund received from the prisoners?

A. I could not answer that without looking up that account.

Q. State how much more you have except that which you took from Mr. Sanders, $2,300, I think. •

A. Yes, sir; $2,200, I think. That is all I have.

Q. None other?

A. No, sir; none other at all.

Q. Don't you owe a man named Grateguth about $135?

A. It is in the cash account.

Q. You owe him this money yet according to the books?

A. Yes.

Q, Did you examine this and see whether it was correct or not? [Referring to Exhibit "B."]

A. Well, now some of these things I don't know about. There is one account here that I would like to look up; that of Payne & Ragsdale, $786.25. Captain Huett figured that up. (Mr. Huett, interrupting, says: "That is the true and correct account of the bills in the office, to my knowledge, when I was asked to make it up by the Senate Committee, outside of the last item.")

Q. State, Captain, if you know anything is incorrect, and whether you owe any other parties outside of this last item?

A. I said I did not think of anything, but that Seymour Mills; that is this $1,025.33.

Q. State if you did not give a note about two years ago for $3,000 to a Loan Association, with Mr. Craig as security, and others?

A. I think I borrowed $3,000; don't think it was two years ago.

Q. Was it not about the time the Committee came down here, and borrowed for the purpose of making up your balance?

A. No, sir; I do not understand that it was. I don't remember a great deal about it.

Q. Do you remember about the amount, and that the note is still unpaid?

A. Oh, I have been paying in weekly payments.

Q. How much is due yet?

A. I do not know, sir.

Q. Does that money belong to the State?

A. No, sir; not as I recollect.

Q. The question I wish to ask, if you borrowed that money for the purpose of making up your shortage at that time?

A. Well, I don't remember what that transaction was exactly.

Q. Was it not when the committee came down'here and you were short that much and you borrowed it?

A. I don't think I borrowed that money at that time at all. I could not say certain.

Q. In reference to that $1,000 that we asked if you had received from Perin & Gaff, or Samuel II. Perin, last Saturday, what is your answer to-day?

A. I got $1,000 from him as a personal advancement. I mean as a personal favor to me.

Q. Is it not a fact that they owe the State about $6,000 ?

A. Yes, more than that ; about $9,000.

Q. Was that an individual transaction ?

A. Yes, sir ; it was.

Q. Why did not they pay it on the $9,000 that they owed.

A. Because they did not propose to pay that $9,000. They have not proposed to pay that, as I explained to you.

Q. My understanding is the claim is $7,000?

A. Yes.

Q. That leaves a difference of $2,000.

A. The reason I have not sued was because I thought that claim would go to the Legislature and be adjusted there. They say they are willing to pay the balance of that account if they can have credit for the $7,000.

Q. State if that $1,000 they let you have was to be applied to that account.

A. No, sir, it was not. I did not so understand it.

Q. I will ask you if you owe any business men about the city or any place for supplies that you have received that are not paid for, outside of those mentioned in Exhibit "C?"

A. Not that I know of. I presume that statement is correct. Allow me to say that in the purchase of supplies for this month some bills are not in there, but prior to that time the bills are all in, as I understand it. My clerk made up that list, and I depend upon him.

Q. Are the coal bills all in?

A. Down to the balance of this month.

Q. Do you get a bill for coal every month?

A. Yes, sir.

Q. I understand you have accounted for this $2,200 of Mr. Sanders on the prison cash book. Your book shows you are indebted on that account $3,645.21 on your convict cash book account. Now that includes the $2,200 of Mr. Sanders's money?

A. No, sir, that don't.

[Question asked of Captain Huett: Is this Grateguth's account included in this $3,645? A. Yes, sir, everything is included in that, with the exception of the $2,200.]

Q. How much money have you on hand?

A. Well, gentlemen, I do not propose to answer that except from the books.

Q. What is your reason for not answering it now? You answered it to the Senate Committee.

A. I want to stand on the investigation of this Committee as to what amount I have on hand. Allow me to say that when you say that the Warden is short all the bills that have not been receipted for you charge him with a shortage that is not there. The State has not paid.

Q. Is it not true when you make your settlement and draw your money out of the Auditor of State's Office, that your appropriations run from one fiscal year to the other, and don't you get the use of the money on that account? In other words, . es?

A. Well, I don't know how the Auditor runs that appropriation business.

Q. Your report shows a balance to your credit of $2,665.33.

A. I drew that on the 27th or 28th of December.

Q. Please explain how much money you have drawn from the State Government since October 31.

A. [By Clerk.] $3,222.22 on this year past.

Q. Is that all that has been drawn within the last two years under the appropriation of the Legislature, the $2,665.33 and the $3,222.2_?

A. No, I drew from the appropriations more than that.

Q. How was your account when you were re-elected Warden?

A. My account was just exactly as my reports show.

Q. Did not your appropriation end at the end of the fiscal year two years ago?

A. No, sir; I want to say that the balance of the appropriation is carried forward to pay the balance of the expenses that has not yet been reported.

Q. Captain, state how much money you have on hand as Warden at the present time.

A. Gentlemen, I submit to you the books of the prison to ascertain how much I should have on hand.

Q. State whether you will answer the question—I will put it this way: How much you have on hand and to produce it for the examination of this Committee?

A. I will not answer that question now. I would like to have you go on with your investigation. I decline to answer that question.

Q. Do you desire to answer it at all?

A. Well, that is a matter I refer to my attorney.

Q. By Mr. Alexander: Why, as Warden, have you not paid the guards here since the 31st of October?

A. We have been two or three months behind for years in the payment of guards. Ever since the prison was idle we have run it two months behind.

Q. By Mr. Patten: Where do you keep your account, as Warden—what bank?

A. Well, I don't keep any particular bank account. When I deposit at all I deposit at the Citizens' National Bank here, and have for the past twenty years.

Q. Any other place ?

A. No, sir.

Q. I will ask you to produce your stub book, and also your check book or pass book, for the examination of this Committee.

A. Until I consult my attorney I will not produce it.

Q. By Mr. Alexander: When convicts die and they have accounts to their credit, what becomes of that money ?

A. Well, that remains to their credit, and we give it to any friends of theirs. If the man has a wife we give it to her.

Q. If their friends never claim the money, then what becomes of it?

A. It remains in the Warden's hands.

Q. Do you know how much of that fund you have on hand?

A. No, sir.

Q. Ask the Clerk if he knows what becomes of that money, if it is accounted for at all.

A. [By Clerk.] It is to their credit on the ledger; in that general convict cash-book.

AFTERNOON SESSION, February 18.

Captain A. J. Howard tendered his resignation to the Directors, who were present, and delivered the following statement in writing to the chairman of the Committee :

" *To the Committee Appointed by the Legislature of the State of Indiana to Examine the Affairs of the Southern State Prison :*

" As Warden of the Southern State Prison of the State of Indiana, I am willing to and do admit that the books of the Southern State Prison show a larger amount due the State, greater than I can now account for and more than I am able or willing to pay, believing, as I do, that the books are incorrect and that I am entitled to credits which the books do not show."

The resignation was accepted by the Directors.

M. I. Huett, being duly sworn, testified as follows :

Q. By Mr. Patten: You are the clerk ?

A. Yes, sir.

Q. Did you make up that statement of expenditures since December 31 ?

A. Yes, sir.

Q. What does that include?

A. We have vouchers for these?

Q. That is all paid out since Dec. 31, 1886?

A. Yes, sir. As to Perin & Gaff items, I want to say it won't show up on Contractors' Book, but I have a small ledger of mine that will show that up. You see, under that law, as I understand it, no one firm can hire more than 100 convicts, and while the Perin & Gaff Mfg. Co. are known as a firm, we keep the accounts separately. On the 31st day of October Mr. Sam. Perin's account closed. That left the accounts of the firm then with Frank L. Perin and Thomas Gaff, and on the 30th day of November Frank Perin went out, and left the account open with Thomas Gaff, and Perin & Gaff Mfg. Co. up to January 15, and after January 15 the account is kept with Perin & Gaff Mfg. Co. You will find no day book of the Patten Mfg. Co. I have report made to me daily, but I know nothing of the correctness of it.

Q. How much do Perin & Gaff owe you now?

A. In the neighborhood of $8,000.

Q. By Mr. Sinclair: Have you furnished us all the books that you have in connection with these accounts?

A. Yes, sir. I want to impress upon your minds, gentlemen, that I am only a subordinate. Captain Howard is Warden. Everything that is done and is to be done is under supervision of Captain Howard. If there are any more receipts for month of January or February than on that book [pointing to cash book] I don't know it.

Statement by Mr. A. J. Howard: To explain why the prison earnings have been a little short, the line of contracts with Perin & Gaff Manufacturing Company have been expiring, and they have been moving out of the prison. The contracts expired at different times. They commenced going out on the first of November.

Q. By Mr. Patten: How much do Perin & Gaff owe you?

A. About $9,000, but they claim $7,000 against the State, and hold back payments on account of that. They proposed to present that claim to this Legislature, and by casting up the contracts I wouldn't make anything for the State.

Q. How is it that February receipts run so much ahead of January if the contracts are expiring?

A. The Perin & Gaff Manufacturing Company didn't pay me anything in January. They paid me $300 in next month. They paid up pretty well in December, keeping back what I tell you. They claimed they would fight the State in a lawsuit.

Q. By Mr. Alexander: What have Perin & Gaff paid you in February?

A. Perin & Gaff have not paid more than what is on that book, $300.

Q. Haven't they or one of them paid more than that in the last month?

A. No, sir.

Q. Is it not a fact that $1,000 was paid last Saturday, either by Perin or Perin & Gaff Manufacturing Company, or by Gaff himself?

A. Well, I don't know. I will look that up. I presumed the clerk put everything on there. •

Q. Why is it that the books are not posted for January?

A. The board has not met to act upon them.

Mr. Huett recalled. FEBRUARY 18.

Q. By Mr. Patten: State if you ever kept any record of the amount of bread from the prison that was used by the Warden or Deputy Warden?

A. No, sir, I never have.

Q. State if Mr. Allen, the Steward, ever made any reports to you of the amounts?

A. Yes; he has at times, and I communicated the report to Captain Howard and he would say it was all right. He would say, "That is all right; I will attend to that." It was never put on the books.

Q. How many years has that matter been going on?

A. If you will look back on the cash book I think you will find, in 1882, where Captain Howard paid some money into the treasury, on account of provisions, but since that time he has paid nothing that I know of.

Q. Do you know how much bread they use? How many barrels of flour a month that is taken out?

A. No, I could not say. I have, time and time again, noticed bread going out day after day, but I don't know where it went. I never kept account of anything that went out.

Q. Is there any money on hand in this institution?

A. I do not know of any.

Q. Any in the safe?

A. I have not access to the safe.

Q. Who is this boy that will be pardoned out to-morrow.

A. Walter Hurt.

Q. It is your duty to pay these men when discharged?

A. Yes, sir.

Deputy Warden Baxter called.

Q. By Mr. Patten : Have you any money belonging to the State?

A. No, sir, I have no State funds at all.

FEBRUARY 19.

Mr. Huett recalled.

Statement: I just saw Captain Howard, and I said to him— says I, "Captain Howard, for God's sake, if you don't pay back any money, do pay back the money you borrowed from that convict. It is a matter of justice and it is a matter of right, and the man ought to have his money;" and I told him I wanted it, and here it is—$2,200. I want to put it before the Committee. And he requested that Captain Baxter give him a receipt for it, he being Acting Warden.

Captain Sanders recalled.

Statement: I want to have it put in bank and see the certificate of deposit.

The money was turned over by the Committe to the Deputy Warden, Mr. Baxter, Acting Warden.

Further examination of Mr. Huett.

By Mr. Alexander :

Q. I wish to ask you about the beef.

A. About the beef? I am never here in the morning when it comes.

Do you know where it comes from—from Louisville?

A. Yes, sir—that is, recently. This is only hearsay; I don't know who I heard it from, but from guards I think; if I understood it right that meat had been delivered here and that George Howard in some way got the benefit of a portion of it, in what way I can't tell.

Q. What do you know about any rebate being made.

A. I don't know one single thing about it.

Q. Did you ever hear the Warden say anything about it or any of his employes?

A. No, sir.

Q. Do you know how much was paid per pound for the beef?

A. The bill states 6 cents.

Q. If it was 6 cents a pound you would know how much beef had been furnished in a certain time.

A. The vouchers will show that the bills came in for sometimes thirteen rations and sometimes fourteen rations. I think fourteen rations was the usual amount per month, and if I recollect aright, the ration cost something like $42—700 pounds a ration.

Q. What do you think about the beef contract; do you think there is any rebate?

A. I think there is a rebate there.

Q. By Mr. Pleak: How do you think it is managed?

A. Well, I could not tell you that. I know that Mr. Allen attends to that meat business, and I know that whenever (nine times out of ten) a check for the meat was delivered, it was delivered to Mr. Allen. Now, how much the rebate was, if there was any, I don't know.

Q. By Mr. Osborne: Was the meat re-weighed when it got here?

A. I don't know.

Q. Did you have any means of re-weighing it here?

A. I don't know. I suppose surely they would, but I don't know that it ever was.

Q. By Mr. Alexander: If there was any rebate, who do you suppose got the benefit of this money?

A. If there was any rebate, I suppose Captain Allen got the benefit of it.

Q. By Mr. Osborne: How long have you been here?

A. Seven years, not counting the time I was away.

Q. When were the wagon scales outside taken away?

A. Four years ago.

Q. By Mr. Pleak: Do you know the price they paid for coal?

A. I think 10 cents.

Q. By Mr. Alexander: What is your best impression—that there was not a rebate on everything?

A. I don't know; I should suppose there was, because I don't think, if there was not something to be made outside of the Warden's salary, that he could live on his salary.

Q. State whether he has been extravagant in his living.

A. I couldn't say that. Well, a man occupying as high position as he does must spend, and he has a family there, and I think entertains a good deal.

Q. Does he have any large parties?

A. No, I can't say that he does.

Q. What is your best impression as to supplies that were furnished him to live on—as to whether he bought them. or whether he took the provisions and supplies that belonged to this institution?

A. I am just giving my impression; I think a great deal of the provisions that went to the Warden's and Deputy Warden's houses was from here.

Q. You don't know of their ever accounting for anything that went from here?

A. No, sir.

Q. You never heard of their charging themselves up with it and settling with the Directors?

A. No, sir.

Q. What do you know about the Directors visiting the prison every month?

A. Oh, they have never done that. They just meet when they have to pass on the accounts.

Q. State what else they do.

A. Well, they audit the accounts. They go to the prison and listen to the complaints of prisoners.

Q. Is it not a fact that when prisoners make complaints before them, don't they then bring in the guards and persons connected with the institution and hear their side, and don't they take their side of the case in preference to that of the convicts'.

A. My impression is that a convicts's word does not go very far with them.

Q. By Mr. Patten: Have you any knowledge of any arrangement between the contractors and Directors here in which there has been money consideration; that the Directors had been paid by these contractors?

A. No, sir; I do not know of any. Never had any reason to believe there is any.

Q. Have you any reason for believing that there was between the Warden and the contractors?

A. Well, I don't know how to answer that question. I don't hardly think there is. I don't know.

Q. State if such a thing as that should occur, could you detect it through your book-keeping?

A. Oh, yes; I think I could, sir.

Q. Then, if there was any arrangement, without your knowledge, it would have to be outside?

A. Yes, sir.

Q. By Mr. Alexander: At the time the Directors met here and elected the Warden the last time, what, if anything, was said about his giving additional bond? Did you give any bond, or the Deputy Warden? What was said about it at the time?

A. I think that the question of bond came up, and I think that the Warden spoke of it on one or two occasions. Says he: "I will have to get up a new bond," and, if I recollect aright, I think the Directors asked him to do so. I think they did.

Q. Do you have to be re-elected at the same time the Warden is?

A. Well, the clerk is elected indefinitely. The Warden said, whenever the question was brought up, he said he was the only one elected for a definite time.

Q. At the time they met here and he was re-elected, you say there was something said about his giving a bond; what steps were taken in regard to it?

A. I do not think any steps were taken; not to my knowledge.

Q. The minutes would show, wouldn't they?

A. I could not say that.

Q. How many bonds have you filed?

A. Two, I think. I have not filed a bond since I came back.

Q. Do you know you have to file a bond for $10,000?

A. I did so seven years ago. My bond is with the Treasurer of State now, with ten and a-half millions represented on it.

Q. Did Captain Baxter file a bond when he was elected Deputy Warden?

A. Yes, sir; on the 15th of September.

Q. You say there was talk about his giving additional bond—do you know of any reason why it was not done?

A. No, sir.

Q. Did you ever hear the Directors say anything about it?

A. No, sir; I think Captain Howard called my attention to the necessity of his filing bond. I don't know what they ever said to him about it.

Q. At the time the Directors met and elected a Warden, would it not be your place to make minutes of the meeting?

A. I thought so, but he would never allow me to. The only minutes I made up would be at unimportant meetings. At important meetings I was never allowed to make up the minutes.

Q. Was anything ever said about your staying out?

A. No; I never was invited.

Q. Has the Board a secretary?

A. I believe Mr. Horn is secretary. If he is absent they have secretary pro tem.

Q. Were their meetings secret?

A. Why, lately, since I got back from Lawrenceburg, Mr. Horn has always insisted on my being present.

Q. You left for Lawrenceburg; when did you come back?

A. I came back the 1st of last March.

Q. Have you filed a bond since you came back?

A. No, sir.

Q. Did you go to stay away when you left?

A. No, sir; I can not say I left permanently. Another clerk was appointed pro tem. I thought if I did not like it I would come back. My salary as Chief Deputy at Lawrenceburg was worth $2,000, here I am only getting $1,000. That seems like a very strange proceeding, and I wish to explain it. When I went to Lawrenceburg, I got there with my family on the 12th day of August. On the 12th day of January my adopted daughter died. After she died, my wife became homesick and heart-broken and wanted to come back here, and, of course, I could not afford to stay there, she and the rest of the family feeling that way. I have this property here; I could not rent it to advantage. I was paying $200 a year rent up there, and then, when I came back here, what I made over and above my salary of $1,000.

Q. How did you make that?

A. I made it selling goods to convicts. He gave me the privilege of selling goods to convicts. I suppose I make—maybe average—$20 to $25 a month. If I had been getting $5,000 at Lawrenceburg I could not afford, with the discontent in my family, to have remained.

Q. At these meetings were you present at Mr. Horn's suggestion or at his request?

A. I was present at his request when they compared accounts. Their other business I had nothing to do with. I usually retired then.

Q. Did they ever say anything about your retiring?

A. No, sir.

Q. Did Howard ever say anything as to your going out or staying out?

A. No, sir.

Q. Did his talk ever indicate to you that he would rather you would be away than present?

A. Well, if I thought my presence was not needed or agreeable, I would not stay.

Q. Did they ever have any private conversation with you, while he was in here?

A. No, sir; not that I know of.

Q. What was the general line of business in looking over the accounts when they had meetings, for instance, in looking over bills?

A. They never inquired any about the money that was on hand. I think they went over the bills pretty thoroughly.

Q. Did they ever examine your books or ask you when Captain Howard was not present?

A. No, sir. On frequent occasions, and they will bear me out, I have called their attention to the manner in which the books are kept, and that they were not kept as I should keep them, but, of course, I had nothing to do only to obey the orders of the Warden. For instance, I remember on one occasion when Captain Horn called the attention of Dr. Wilson to this fact. That was after I had spoken to Captain Horn. Says he, "Doctor, this is the cash book, isn't it?" He says, "Yes." "Well," says he, "do you think when we come here and audit these bills that the vouchers as shown here on the cash book, representing bills, do you think they are all paid?" Dr. Wilson

said, "Why, yes: of course." "Well," he says, "they are not."
Then they said that must not be so: that must be looked into,
or something to that effect.

Q. Is it not true that there are bills represented here that
they audited as paid that really were not paid?

A. My goodness, yes; month after month. Now, although
there is a reflection east upon me, I believe I know how to
keep books. Now, if any of you gentlemen understand anything about book-keeping, supposing the books were audited
to-day, the cash-book was thrown open. Of course the debit
side will show the receipts and the credit side the disbursements. It don't do it here. Suppose I take any one man's
account—say Eakin's account—and posted it from the cash-
book to ledger as being paid when it was not paid, wouldn't
that have been a fraudulent entry? That was the reason I
did not keep a ledger. On the morning the Senate Committee
was here, which statement can be corroborated, I paid a bill of
$425 to Mr. Harvey McCampbell, the president of the Second
National Bank, that was audited last March. Supposing I had
entered that account last March when it was audited, would
that have been a true exhibit of that man's account? It could
not be.

Q. Did you ever inform the Directors that some of these
bills audited paid were not paid; that they audited them as
paid when they were not paid?

A. Yes, sir; I have.

Q. By Mr. Patten: How often did you notify them?

A. Oh, I don't know how many times.

Q. Very often? Sufficient for them to have taken account
of it?

A. Yes, sir.

Q. By Mr. Alexander: How long has that been going on
since they had notice of it?

A. Ever since they had office.

Q. Did these transactions extend over any length of time?

A. Well, take the salary account, it was never paid until
two or three months after, but they audited it on the credit
side of the cash-book.

Q. That has been the system ever since the present Directors were in office?

A. Yes, sir.

Q. By Mr. Patten: Who directed you to keep the account that way?

A. Captain Howard.

Q. When you called his attention to the necessity of keeping a ledger account, can you state what his instructions were?

A. Well, every entry made on there was by his order. Sometimes, as the Directors can tell you, the cash-book would not be made up until after they had been here half a day, sometimes a day. He would call me and say: "Well, what vouchers have you got that are paid?" I would give him the list. "For what month do we owe Eakin or Sparks?" I would give him the accounts, and then he would put them in to augment, to increase the debit side of cash when they were not paid.

Q. By Mr. Alexander: About this convict fund. I see from the books that it is represented that a number of convicts take a paper called the "Jeffersonville Times;" what do you know about prisoners being compelled to take that paper?

A. I could not say that any of the prisoners were compelled to take it, but know that Martin, the Librarian, was in the habit of going around among the convicts and taking subscriptions for the Times, as the books will show.

Q. What do you know about any false entries in regard to prisoners taking the Times, when they did not order it?

A. There never was a spurious entry in that convict account. I know that because I have exclusive control over that business. That is, the man goes around and brings me the orders. That is all I know about it. I have an order for every entry on the book.

Q. By Mr. Pleak: What is your best impression of the number of copies of the Times taken by the convicts?

A. I suppose about in the neghborhood of fifty.

Q. About that number regularly?

A. Well, it fluctuates. Sometimes the subscriptions are larger; sometimes not so much.

Q. By Mr. Alexander: When the Directors would come here, and they would know some of these bills were not paid and audited as paid, did they ever examine your books?

A. No, sir.

Q. What do you know about their ordering the business done differently than what it had been?

A. They never did. They never ordered it made in any way.

Q. Just went on in the same way?

A. Yes, sir.

Q. By Mr. Patten: In reference to what is called the visitors' fund, state the manner of receiving that fund and accounting for it.

A. That fund has been handled by three of four men. That is the way of selling tickets. When I sold a ticket I kept an account of it, and all the tickets that went into that box that I sold I made account of to the Warden.

Q. How?

A. I would give him the money.

Q. Did you make any book account?

A. There is a small book account of it.

Q. Did you just lump it at the end of the day?

A. Every month, not daily. That visitors' fund, if every person had been charged that went in, of course, would be a pretty large amount, but I know of many instances where parties of forty and fifty went through and never paid a cent.

Q. State how you kept account of that fund.

A. I kept it in a small side book.

Q. You paid the money as it came into your hands to the Warden?

A. Yes, sir.

Q. Then you say others sold the tickets?

A. Yes.

Q. Who took up the money?

A. I don't know anything about that.

Q. Who else sold?

A. Sometimes Mr. Bellew, a guard.

Q. What did he do with the money?

A. I can not say as to that; I have received money from him and accounted for it with mine.

Q. How many tickets were sold outside of your office?

A. I don't know; it was a loose way; anybody has access to the office.

Q. And when the tickets were sold and were deposited in the boxes, then you went out there and took these tickets out of the box?

A. Yes, sir, I always found my tickets there; the tickets always corresponded with my cash.

Q. I understood you to say there were two boxes.

A. No, sir, there is only one box.

Q. If you found scattered tickets in there—say you had only received pay for twenty-five tickets, did you just give credit for twenty-five tickets?

A. Why, on two or three occasions I found, maybe all in all, twenty-five tickets, if I recollect aright, that could not be accounted for, and I know that my account was right. I called Captain Howard's attention to it, and he said he did not know anything about it; he would see to it.

Q. Then, when you found an excess number of tickets, you only accounted for your own?

A. Only those I was personally accountable for.

Q. What about your safe?

A. The safe is worth about a quarter of a dollar. I want to say I never had access to this safe. Of course, I called his attention to it in the placing of the books.

Q. In case of fire, the books would be totally destroyed?

A. It looks to me that way. I had a racket with him several times about it. I called his attention to the books being exposed, and almost daily here lately, a convict was allowed to go and look at my convict ledger and see how the different accounts of the men stood. I don't know for what reason it was done. I suppose it was to see whether the men had money enough to buy papers, and I told him that there was no security. Instead of being in the safe as they ought to be, they are allowed to remain exposed and accessible to anybody.

Q. The Warden, in answer to a question to state and produce the amount of cash he had on hand, made the following reply: "As Warden of the Southern State Prison of the State of Indiana, I am willing to and do admit that the books of the Southern State Prison show a larger amount due the State greater than I can now account for and more than I am able or willing to pay, believing, as I do, that the books are incorrect, and that I am entitled to credits which the books do not show." What have you to say to that?

A. In answer to that, I will state emphatically and positively that these books were kept just as they were found, according to his knowledge and order, and that is the truth, gentlemen.

Q. By Mr. Sinclair: Have you any separate book of your own by which you would know better how things stood than you did with these present books?

A. I have a ledger—Mr. Coons has it—that I got up for my own benefit to know how these contractors stood. That is the small book with the red back. So that I could see, for instance, what we owed Eakin or what the contractors owed us. It was impracticable to keep a ledger from the loose way of business we had. I could not make a ledger account of an account that was paid on one book, and was not paid, could I?

Q. You kept this private book for your own special benefit, to see what you were doing?

A. Yes, sir.

Q. And you kept these other books just as Howard said?

A. Yes, sir.

Q. By Mr. Alexander: This underclothing that you sell, we have heard some complaint of its being sold for two prices?

A. I can show you the underclothing I have. Of course, I want to make a little money, but then I would not be extortionate on the prisoners, and they will bear me out; nine out of ten will state to you I have sold very reasonable. Take the article of soap: it costs me on an average sixteen cents for three bars. I sell that for twenty-five cents. They are not bound to buy from me. I see in some paper where the convicts had stated that goods coming here for them, in our care, had never been turned over. I most solemnly swear that all goods that have come for any convict I turned over to them.

Q. By Mr. Patten: What is the reason a box of goods sent to Mr. Mayfield, from Sullivan County, was kept for four or five weeks and then returned?

A. They might have been contraband goods: for instance, eatables or oranges; the Warden will not allow them inside. I can solemnly swear that any article of clothing that ever came, to my knowledge, I sent for the man and gave it to him.

Q. What is done with the contraband goods?

A. I don't know. I think they are generally sent back. I can state that everything that comes in my possession I put in a drawer over there and label it.

Q. What about these unopened letters?

A. I only open letters during the absence of the Warden, and then only letters that are addressed to him as Warden.

M. I. Huette recalled.

Q. By Mr. Patten : What do you know about this brick-yard account?

A. Before I came here as Clerk, if I recollect aright, on the 31st day of May, there was $6,000 paid over by Col. Merry-weather, but there have been debits and credits on that account, I should think, to four years ago; and then all I know is what Captain Howard told me, that there was about $2,700 or $2,800 unaccounted for, but I have not seen that brick-yard book for some time: but the receipts and disbursements on that account run over $6,000—twice that much, I guess. Mr. Coons, when he made up his balance-sheet, estimated it at $3,000, and it seems that he had made an arrangement to meet Captain How-ard and discuss this business; and on the Saturday he was over the river, in the evening when he came back, I told him that Captain Howard had asked to see him, and he made some kind of reply that, "Oh, I guess he did not want to see me." Then he said, instead of estimating the brick-yard account at $3,000 he guessed he had better estimate it at $5,000. I told him I did not know anything about the brick-yard account; that I would not be surprised if he could estimate it at that.

Q. You have not got that brick-yard book?

A. No, sir, I guess it is at Captain Howard's house. He took books, papers, etc., away from here, and took them to his house.

Q. State if you know anything about what was done with the cats used in the prison.

A. I never saw these cats but once. This Directors' room then was a store-room, and I used to see Captain Craig come here every day or so. I knew very well what he came in for, because on several occasions I heard the men halloo in punish-ment, and knew what he did, although I never saw it. The only time I saw the cat was about four years ago. There was an investigating committee here, and there were some ladies with the committee, and—well, they were exhibited to these ladies, and I saw them.

Q. By Mr. Alexander: How long ago is it since cats have been used?

A. I think it is four years this March.

Q. By Mr. Patten: Why did they cease to use cats?

A. I could not tell you about that. I suppose from the way Captain Howard always talked that it was through his instrumentality that they were abolished, by reason of having this good-time law passed.

Q. How many cats did they have, a big and a small one?

A. I only saw one.

Q. How long was that?

A. I should judge the strips on it were about eighteen inches; the whole concern was about three feet or so.

Q. State if you know of any transaction between Captain Howard and Col. Shay, in reference to an envelope.

A. Yes, sir, I have seen the envelope. I saw the envelope about two and a half years ago.

Q. How was it directed?

A. If I recollect aright it was addressed "Col. Thomas Shay. Private." I think that was the only indorsement there was on it.

Q. Did it contain anything?

A. Oh, yes; it had some papers in it. I think it was a yellow envelope, and I suppose it contained papers, about one-quarter of an inch thick.

Q. Did you handle it?

A. Well, in passing over envelopes, I handled it; yes, sir. I never knew the contents of it. It was sealed.

Q. What relation did Col. Shay have to this institution?

A. He was a Director in 1879. He was here about two years, I think. The Directors were Col. Shay and Mr. Linck and P. L. D. Mitchell, from Bloomington.

Q. State if you knew anything as to what the envelope contained.

A. I don't know. I have an impression that it contained matters relating to the cell-house.

Q. Was that new cell-house being constructed at that time?

A. Well, I saw this envelope after the cell-house was completed.

Q. State about the time it was completed.

A. I think the cell-house was constructed in 1884. Sweeney & McCormick were the contractors on the cell-house.

Q. What did Colonel Shay have to do with it?

A. Well, I don't know what he had to do with it that time. I know there was a great deal of discussion going on, and the Sweeney Bros. were here and Mr. McCormick was here.

Q. Was there any money drawn out—do the books show Colonel Shay received any money at that time ?

A. No, sir.

Q. Do you know whether that envelope contained money ?

A. I could not say that it did.

Q. Did you make any papers or reports to be sent to Colonel Shay ?

A. No, sir, I never did.　　　　　　　　　　　　　　·

Q. Was he chairman of the Board of Directors, or did they have any chairman ?

A. They never did until here lately. I think he was the senior member of the Board.

Q. By Mr. Alexander: Did you ever have any conversation with Captain Howard about that envelope ?

A. Captain Howard never told me anything about it. I don't want to do the man any injustice at all, but then I suppose it was matters pertaining to this cell-house business. I don't know the nature of the papers. I want to say, gentlemen, that on Saturday Mr. McCampbell, president of the National Bank. I had passed the bank on the opposite side of the street, and he called me back, Friday or Saturday, I think Saturday, and he says, " Captain, do you know anything about that acceptance of Patten & Co." " Why," says I, " I don't know what you are talking about." Neither did I. He wanted to know if that transaction was legitimate. Says I, " I don't known what you are talking about." He says, " Oh, I thought maybe you knew all about it. There was an acceptance in favor of Captain Howard by the Patten Manufacturing Company. Did not you get him some drafts ? " I told him Mr. Allen, for Captain Howard, asked me to get some blank drafts at the Citizens' National and also at the other National, and I did so and gave them in blank. " Well, that was what it was, and I wanted to know if that was all right." I said, " I can tell you the Patten Manufacturing Company is a legitimate firm ; whether that transaction was legitimate or not, I do not know." Now, what that transaction was I do not know.

Q. Do you know the amount?

A. I won't be certain but what he said $2,000.

Q. Who is the superintendent of the Patten Mfg. Co. ?

A. Wm. D. Patten.

W. D. Patten, being first duly sworn, testified as follows :

Q. By Mr. Patten: Mr. Huette make your statement, as above. Now, I wish you to state, Mr. Patten, what transaction you had with Captain Howard in reference to that matter?

A. I have not had any transaction with Captain Howard.

Q. Did you advance him any money?

A. No, sir, I did not; I advanced no money to the State to any one, nor to any of the officials.

Q. When did you start in on your contract?

A. We virtually started in on the 1st of January.

Q. How much have you paid in?

A. We have not paid anything in. I have mentioned once or twice I would like to have a bill for the labor, but never had. Mr. Huette said he called Captain Howard's attention to it, and he said he would see about it. The last time anything was said about money, I think it was a few days before this committee came here. The Captain spoke about money then, and I told him we were ready to pay whenever the bills were presented to us.

David M. Allen, having been duly sworn, testified as follows:

Q. By Mr. Patten: State what position you hold in this prison?

A. I am Steward.

Q. State if you purchase the supplies of the institution?

A. I do, under the order and directions of the Warden.

Q. Where do you purchase your beef?

A. Of a man named Bloom, in Louisville, for last year and a half.

Q. Before that time who did you purchase of?

A. Of a man named John Duff, in Louisville.

Q. State what kind of beef you buy?

A. This man Bloom is what is called a wholesale butcher, kills from six to eight. He sells the loin and standing ribs to the steamboats and to the hotels, and we get the balance. We get the brisket and the shoulder and the balance of the beef except the loin, rib and round, that is, one part of the round.

Q. What price do you have to pay for beef?

A. Six cents a pound.

Q. Is that a first-class price?

A. That is.

Q. Can not you buy beef from any other point, or from the same point, at the same price without any select parts being taken away?

A. No, sir; I think not. We tried to butcher here when Captain Howard first became Warden, and it is an actual fact that this kind of beef Bloom sells is worth 3¾ to 4 cents on foot, and it takes a good steer to net 50 per cent.; 55 per cent. is an extra steer. Then the butcher has the head and tail.

Q. State if any of that beef is ever used by any of the officers of this Institution, taken out without being accounted for?

A. No, sir.

Q. Do they occasionally take beef?

A. No, sir.

Q. By Mr. Osborn: Do the butchers furnish them beef on their own account?

A. Captain Howard buys his beef here at Fisher's, and has never had a pound of beef from Bloom since he has furnished it. Captain Craig at one time bought beef for his boarding house, but that was separate and distinct; that was his private business. It never entered in our account, and I never furnished any beef from the prison ration.

Q. You were in the habit of going on fishing junkets?

A. Yes, sir.

Q. Did you do that at the expense of the State?

A. Not by a long shot.

Q. Wouldn't it be very convenient to do so?

A. Well, yes. The only thing the State ever had. We borrowed our blankets from the prison, but always packed them in a nice box. The State furnished that. We would go out in May and October, twice a year, and we would borrow the blankets.

Q. Didn't you usually make it convenient to buy your provisions for the fishing party from some house that you had patronized for prison supplies?

A. Well, yes, sir, I would go and buy them at wholesale.

Q. Don't you reckon you made a mistake sometimes and charged it up to the State?

A. Never in the world, sir.

Q. Are you clear?

A. I am as clear as I can be.

Q. You bought a great many hams from Eakin & Co.?

A. Yes, sir, I bought half a dozen hams on one occasion and half a dozen sides of breakfast bacon.

Q. Did you have that charged on your own account?

A. I did. When we got back we put the bills together, and Captain Craig paid his half and I my half.

Q. You are familiar with the report and rumor?

A. Gentlemen, I have been around. The report and rumor was that there never was any honest man connected with this Institution.

Q. What is your opinion on that?

A. My opinion is, gentlemen, that we are lied on.

Q. State how it happens that the bread is baked in this prison and taken to the Deputy Warden's and Warden's.

A. Well, it has been the custom ever since I have been Steward, and that is twelve years, to bake bread for the Warden and Deputy Warden and charge them up with the flour.

Q. Who charges it?

A. I will tell you how. They will furnish the flour, for instance, and I will bake the bread; I know exactly about how many pounds of bread a barrel of flour makes; I would charge them with the flour and report it to the Clerk.

Q. Why don't that show up on the books?

A. I can not answer that question.

Q. Don't you know as a fact no such account appears on the books?

A. I don't know anything about what appears on the books.

Q. How did you make that report—in writing?

A. Verbally; I told the clerk to charge Captain Howard's account with a barrel of flour.

Q. How often did you do that?

A. Well, I haven't done it for six months, I presume.

Q. How many barrels of flour do they use a week or month?

A. I suppose a barrel of flour would reach Captain Howard's private family two or three months; I am talking about bread for his private family.

Q. How much flour would Mr. Craig use?

A. He would use two barrels of flour every month.

Q. How much is a barrel of flour worth?

A. I think about $4.25; it will average $4.50.

Q. That would be two and a-third barrels a month at $4 a barrel; what is the average?

A. My flour would average during the year about $4.75, perhaps. This is first-class flour.

Q. Were there any other things that went there?

A. Nothing.

Q. Any potatoes?

A. No, sir.

Q. Sugar?

A. No, sir.

Q. Coffee?

A. No, sir.

Q. How much whisky did you buy a month or year?

A. Well, sir, the whisky is bought for the hospital on request of the physician. I don't know. He would give me a bill of drugs and supplies for every month.

Q. Did you buy a barrel for every month?

A. No, sir; I had nothing to do with the buying of the whisky. The Warden would attend to that. I suppose they use two gallons of whisky a month in the hospital.

Q. Not more than that?

A. Perhaps three; owing to the number of patients they had.

Q. Did you buy vegetables for this institution?

A. We did not buy any—only potatoes. The vegetables were raised in the garden.

Q. Is it not a fact that a great amount of potatoes would go from here to Captain Craig or the Warden's?

A. No, sir; it is not. I am sure of that.

Q. You say there is no meat ever furnished directly from this prison to the Warden, Deputy Warden, or taken out by yourself?

A. Yes, sir; I say that. I am positive.

Q. Why has there been no report of bread for the last six months?

A. When Captain Craig was here—I think the last two or three months he was here—he baked most of his bread, or a great portion, at his house. He had reduced the quantity, and when he left here I think they were using two or three barrels of flour that he had bought and sent here that just about squared his account.

Q. Why was it necessary for Mr. Craig to buy two or three barrels of flour of you?

A. From the very fact that I had a class of flour that my bakers could handle and make better bread out of than any flour in the market of the same grade.

Q. You remember when the Senate Investigating Committee was here?

A. Yes.

Q. Can you tell this committee how many barrels of beans you had on hand the day they came down? Don't you remember that you had fourteen barrels.

A. I do not; I bought beans, I think, sometime this month.

Q. How many barrels?

A. I have the invoice bill in the office.

Q. · Were there twenty barrels?

A. No, sir; I don't think so.

Q. State from your best recollection if there was not fourteen barrels of beans on hand when they came?

A. I can not say. I suppose there was twelve to fourteen barrels.

Q. How many of these barrels are on hand now?

A. I don't know. I have not counted them up.

Q. How many barrels do you use a day?

A. The day we use beans twice, we use about $3\frac{1}{2}$ bushels—over a barrel.

Q. The Committee was here on last Friday?

A. Yes, sir.

Q. State if it is not a fact that you hauled out and took away nearly all of those beans, say ten barrels.

A. I have not hauled a barrel out nor taken a bean away.

Q. Why are they not in that store-house?

A. They are there, or they have been consumed every one of them.

Q. By Mr. Pleak: Do you remember what you paid a barrel for the beans?

A. I paid $1.25 a bushel.

Q. By Mr. Alexander: What do you know about the garden; was it kept by the convicts?

A. Yes, sir.

Q. What becomes of the produce?

A. They go inside and to the Warden and Deputy Warden's houses.

Q. What did the convicts get from it during the summer season ?

A. Tomatoes, onions, lettuce, radishes and cabbage.

Q. How often a day ?

A. During abundance of it, three times a day.

Q. By Mr. Patten : Referring to the financial transaction which took place here the other day, will you tell this Committee what part you took in raising about $6,000 or $7,000 to meet the deficiency of the Warden and present before the Senate Committee ?

A. Well, I will tell you, gentlemen. The facts in the case is, Captain Howard came to me, told me he wanted the money raised, said he had arrangements made that failed him and he must have it. I told him " it was d— pretty time to come to me to raise that amount of money. Where am I going to get it. I have got none of my own." He says, " I must have it." I started out into the street, and I drew up a note and began to get names on it, and I was surprised at myself, surprised at the whole transaction. I succeeded in half an hour, went to the bank and put it to his credit. He said, " I only want it for a day or two, as soon as I can make some arrangements." I went and placed it to his credit. I borrowed it on my own motion. I did not ask him what he wanted it for; didn't take his note. I knew Jack Howard was honest and big-hearted, and, if he was in trouble, I would help him out.

Q. You undertook it with the understanding that it was to be a short loan ?

A. It was to be paid the next day or two.

Q. I will ask you if you did not check out $6,000 on Saturday ?

A. No, sir; I checked $7,162.27. He drew the check in there when the Senate Committee was in there, called me to go up town and get this check cashed. I went up town, brought it down and he put it in the safe.

Q. When was this money paid back ?

A. It was paid back on Monday morning. I took $2,000 and Mr. Baxter took the other $5,000.

Q. Give us the facts about raising $3,000 to meet deficiency when the Legislative Committee was here two years ago.

A. He came to me, I think it was put off to the last moment. He said: " By gosh, I must have $3,000." " Well,"

says I, " have you tried to get it anywheres?" He says, "I
have tried, and my efforts have failed; can you raise it?" I
went out, and says I, " Craig, Jack wants us to raise $3,000.
If you will sign this note, I will get the money." He signed
it. I went to the Loan Association, borrowed it out on ten
days' time. At the end of ten days, Captain Jack comes and
says: " How long have you borrowed that money for?" Says
I, " Ten days." Says he, " I can't pay it in that time. I have
got it in my accounts; can't you make that loan longer?" I
saw Craig. Says he, " II—l, we are stuck on that money; see
if you can get that loan." I went to the secretary of the Loan
Association. Says I, " Will you allow me to extend that loan ?"
He says, " Yes, certainly." At the expiration of that loan I
went to him and said, " Captain, you have got to make some
arrangements to meet that Loan Association business, due in a
few days." He says: " Can't you arrange it by getting into
the new association? I have got $500 in the other association;
I will draw that out and pay it, and you can take some shares."
I went up and took the shares, and Craig and I indorsed and gave
him the note and took twenty-five shares. We had to get three
or four indorsers according to the by-laws. I goes to work
and gets four months on it. He has been paying that from
time to time until, I think, he has paid between $900 or $1,000—
I think about $1,500.

Q. How much stock does Howard own in the Jeffersonville
Times?

A. I think he owns it all.

Q. By Mr. Osborn: All the slop goes to feed the Warden's
hogs and cows—does he sell any of them?

A. The hogs—he would have made a spec but the cholera
struck him and knocked thunder out of him. The Warden
can, by close attention, make money by feeding it to the hogs.

Q. Does he sell the refuse from that mill?

A. No, sir, it is consumed right here.

Q. It amounts to some two barrels a day?

A. Oh, no; that Senate Committee made quite a point on
me; they wanted to know what was the difference in cost in
making and buying hominy. I told them I could buy hominy
for $2.70 a barrel and it cost about $2.40 to make it. I says, it
takes six barrels of corn to make a barrel of hominy, but you
take six barrels and you make two hundred pounds of hominy.

Q. By Mr. Hobson: How much hominy do you make on an average, per day?

A. I have to use a barrel a day.

Q. Two barrels of offal a day?

A. Nearly so; yes, sir.

Q. What do you do with the old flour barrels? Is it true that they are sold for 17½ cents each?

A. No, sir, I have sold them at twenty cents.

Q. How many do you have per month?

A. We have about fifty, I suppose.

Q. You sold the bones?

A. Yes, sir.

Q. About how many pounds of that per month?

A. Well, the bones per month would be about 400 or 500 pounds.

Q. You got how much per 100 for them?

A. Sixty cents. That has always been considered the Steward's perquisites—the bones and empty barrels.

Q. By Mr. Alexander: You was here when Mr. Howard was elected Warden the last time?

A. Yes, sir.

Q. What do you know of any money being offered the Directors to vote for him for Warden?

A. That kind of a transaction they didn't count me in.

Q. Was there not any talk about it at the time?

A. No; I have heard this street rumor that some fellow had been bought. There were three or four disappointed candidates.

Q. You never heard Captain Howard say anything about that?

A. No, sir; not a word.

I want to explain in reference to hauling beans. The Senate Committee asked me that question when they came. I told them I never done a transaction of that kind. But two years ago, in 1884, when the water was getting up here, I had 20 or 30 barrels of beans. The Relief Committee came up and said: "I have an order for ten barrels of beans. There ain't a bean in Louisville." Says I: "I can furnish them to you." I loaned them to him, and when he came back he gave me bean for bean for them.

W. P. Barnhill, having been duly sworn, testified as follows :

Q. You are the Chaplain?

A. Yes, sir.

Q. Have you had any Sunday-school lately?

A. Not since I came in.

Q. When was that?

A. I was elected in September. It had been abandoned or discontinued.

Q. What was the reason of its discontinuation?

A. Dissatisfaction and friction in the running of the school.

Q. Have you attempted to reorganize it?

A. I have a school organized I teach on Sunday morning, which I expect will develop into a Sunday-school in a few weeks.

Q. When was that organized?

A. In November.

Q. Have you any regular school where you teach the common branches?

A. This is the school. I teach arithmetic, geography, reading and writing. I have taken illiterate men who could not take part in a general Sunday-school, who needed first to learn this.

Q. What facilities have you for intercourse with the prisoners in the cells?

A. I have access at any time. I put in Sunday evenings and during the week frequently.

Dr. Norvell, having been duly sworn, testified as follows :

Q. By Mr. Patten : Were any pecuniary inducements made to you for the purpose of influencing your vote as Director in the election of a Warden?

A. Well, I have been approached in different ways. I suppose you have reference more particularly to Captain Howard, who was elected Warden. I can plainly answer you just in this way. I am very glad you have asked me this question. Newspaper rumors have been afloat that I received money from Captain Howard, and I saw a hint of that kind in the Cincinnati Enquirer. I want to say to you that I never received one cent from Captain Howard in my life for having voted for him for Warden of this prison. I did not intend to vote for Captain Howard at first. Peter McCarthy had asked me to vote for him some considerable time before. I had promised to do so, and fully intended doing it. I found, however, after coming down here at that meeting, that Dr. Hunter had a candidate in the person of a Mr. Tubbs. Major Finney, who was Republican member on the Board, had a candidate by the name of Neff. Neither of the gentlemen suited me; neither Major Fenney nor Dr. Hunter would vote for McCarthy. Captain Howard always treated me very kindly, and wanted me to vote for him, and I said to Peter McCarthy and others I was going to cast my first vote for Captain Howard. I could not get my man and I did not like the others. I came in and cast my first vote for Captain Howard, and Major Finney having done the same thing, that elected him.

Q. Doctor, state if you received any proposition from any other source?

A. I did. One thing right there; I would like to state this, the gentlemen who approached me with propositions are my friends.

Q. Did anybody us a friend of Captain Howard, or his agent, make any proposition to you?

A. No, sir.

Q. Was Captain Craig at that time a candidate?

A. He was.

Q. Did he make any proposition to you?

A. I don't think he did.

Q. State if there was any proposition coming from him in any direction?

A. I could not say positively that there was not anything of the kind coming from him. I don't have any recollection of Captain Craig making any proposition. He talked to me about being a candidate.

Q. We are talking about a money proposition.

A. I do not know. I have no recollection of Captain Craig offering that kind of a proposition to me.

Q. Do you know of any of his friends making it for him?

A. I would rather not answer that question. I shall have to say frankly that men whom I regarded as his friends were very anxious for his election.

Q. Did they offer any money consideration?

A. Well, I was told I could get money for doing so. I don't know that I was ever offered it. I did not entertain any proposition of the kind, I am sure.

Q. Was there any sum named ?

A. Well, now, Captain, I don't know, certainly, what to say about that.

Q. You can state to the Committee how it was.

A. It has been a good while ago. You see there were, quite a number of applicants, and there were quite a number of gentlemen here in the interest of Mr. Tubbs, and they were ready to make almost any kind of proposition ; some of them had government offices to bestow ; others had a great deal of wealth, but would not name amounts they would pay. You see, men are very particular about giving the amount.

Q. Did anybody offer you money to vote for Captain Craig for Warden ?

A. Well, now, I can't exactly answer that question. I can assure you that no gentleman connected with this institution is being referred to in this conversation at all. The conversation I had was with Capt. Craig's friends. You see, gentlemen, you can not really appreciate the political situation in this locality. There is quite a number of factions, particularly so in the Democratic party, and they fight each other a great deal, and there seems to be a great deal of bad blood existing. There is a very bitter feeling existing between them, more so than between opposite parties.

Q. State if anybody in Jeffersonville, as Craig's friend, offered you any amount of money to vote for Captain Craig.

A. Yes, sir.

Q. I will ask you who that man was?

A. I don't want to get that man in any trouble. You see, Captain Howard was re-elected, and Captain Howard did not give me one cent.

Q. By Mr. Pleak: You are familiar with the duties of Directors in visiting the prison. I would like to ask you if that has been your practice here?

A. No, sir ; not in that particular way. Captain Horn, living near the city, has been here quite often. There was a practice in vogue when I came here for the Board to meet every month. We have all met every month, or at least a sufficient number of us. I have missed, perhaps, three or four or five meetings during the whole term. I have been Director pretty nearly four years.

Q. State if you inspected the accounts of the prison.

A. We inspected the accounts every month.

Q. State the manner of proceeding.

A. In the first place, when we came down here, we would sometimes take the books up first, and sometimes visit the prison first. Sometimes we separated. Ordinarily we got together and passed through all the shops to hear and see the prisoners in the penitentiary, and each prisoner understands that he has the right to speak to us. If he has any complaints of any character, or wishes to come before the Board, he gives us his name, and after we have gone through the prison we fix some time during the time we are here to hear complaints of the prisoners. Captain Horn is Secretary. I am acting as President. We keep notes of what prisoners have to say. Each prisoner is brought in separately, and there is ordinarily nobody in here except the prisoner and the Board of Directors. Then he has the privilege of making any complaints of any character in the world that he wishes to. Then we investigate it in a manner to suit the complaint. When a man is sick we refer him to the physican, and frequently in investigating matters of punishment we bring in guards, but I will say to you candidly that I believe that seventy-five per cent. of the complaints usually made do not amount to anything at all, and, in reality, we know there is a certain class of fellows coming nearly all the time. When any matters require our assistance we always try to make the best of it that we can. Some cases we refer to the Warden, others to the physician. If the complaint was that there was not enough heat in the cell we would speak to the cell guard about it. Sometimes they complained of the food. Ordinarily the man complained that he could not perform his task. Pretty often it is the prisoner's fault, trying to play off. When we wanted to know what the task was we saw the guard and asked what kind of a man that is, and if he can perform that labor he is required to do it. If he is disabled or claims inability for it, we refer him to the physician.

We have three books, one Directors' record, and other larger books in which the accounts are kept and bills filed. Then another made by the clerk—two duplicates on each page. Captain Horn will take one book and the clerk another. Captain Horn will come to this bill, and if there is anything wrong about it we try to correct it. We see if the bills correspond with the book Dr. Wilson has, and corresponds with the voucher I am to sign, when we get through. That is all there is about it.

Q. What can you know about the supplies having been furnished?

A. We can't know very much; we would go into the kitchen sometimes and see what was there. Visiting the prison, a man can not come and stay here but a short time.

Q. By Mr. Alexander: What has been done in regard to investigating the accounts of the Warden, when you met every month?

A. Our investigation is simply to see that the accounts correspond—that they agreed with the minutes of the meetings preceding—and to go through the prison.

Q. Would you ever go back and make any overhauling of his books in any way?

A. I never did go back very far into the books.

Q. Did you try to find out anything about his money account?

A. I know nothing about his money accounts.

Q. Did you examine into the convict fund?

A. No, sir, I can not say that I have; I had no business with it; my understanding was that it was all right.

Q. Did you ever ask him about the amount of money he had on hand belonging to the Institution—have him show up his money?

A. No, I never had him show up his money—anything of that kind. The truth is that it is natural to fall into the plans of men that come before me, and I suppose I felt that way. We thought it was really better for Captain Horn to visit the prison; it was very convenient, and on an average I guess he visited the prison oftener than the law required: I thought that would be sufficient.

Q. By Mr. Pleak: As a rule your visits were rather hasty —a mere cursory view of the accounts.

A. We did up the business as rapidly as we could conveniently: we were here a few days each time; we always stayed a day to look at the accounts, and supposed we were correct before we passed them. All we had—here was the bill, here was the duplicate, and here was the amount on the book. We did not see the meat, we did not see the tobacco, but supposed, as a matter of course, these things had been consumed.

Dr. Norvell recalled.

Q. By Mr. Alexander: A rumor has been before this Committee that at the time of the re-election of the Warden here, Senator Rahm, I believe was the man, in the interest of somebody is said to have telegraphed you this telegram: "I will give you $4,000 for your corn." What have you to say in regard to it?

A. Well, gentlemen, I can answer that question very frankly. I never had a telegram from Senator Rahm in my life on any subject.

Q. Did you from anybody?

A. I have never had a telegram from any individual living on the subject of the election of Warden, that I now remember, and so far as the telegram in regard to corn is concerned, I have never heard of it before, except in conversation with a gentleman day before yesterday, who said there was a rumor of that kind.

Mr. R. J. Wilson, having been duly sworn, testified as follows:

Q. By Mr. Patten: State your relation to the prison.

A. I am one of the Directors.

Q. How long have you been a Director?

A. Something over year; I do not remember the exact date.

Q. State if you have ever been approached by any body since you have been an officer of this prison, in a corrupt manner, for the purpose of influencing your vote.

A. No, sir; I have never helped elect. The Warden was in when I came on the Board. I helped elect the Chaplain, Physician and Deputy Warden. Mr. Horn was on the Board when I came; I succeeded Dr. Hunter, I think, in August.

Q. You was elected to fill his unexpired term?

A. Yes, by Governor Gray. These are the only elections there have been since I was here, and none of those gentlemen offered me anything.

Q. Have you any knowledge of the Warden offering anything at the last election to secure his re-election?

A. No, sir; I don't know anything about that.

Q. State if you had any conversation with Captain Howard or any body that is connected with the prison in reference to any use of money or influence to secure his re-election?

A. No, sir; I don't know anything about that at all.

Q. State, if in your connection with the Clerk here, as an

officer, whether or not you know he has his own system of book-keeping—whether or not he has been interfered with in any manner in keeping his accounts.

A. Not that I know of.

Q. State if he met with your Board, and assisted you in passing on the bills before you.

A. He always was accommodating and gave all the light and information we asked for.

Q. State if the manner of book-keeping in this institution is like that of any other ordinary business.

A. I am not much of a book-keeper.

Q. What was your method of business at these meetings?

A. We went through the prison and heard complaints, and the next thing we had men come here and report to us; send for the guards and investigate the causes of complaint. After we got through with that we went through the bills, and they always compared with the books, and everything looked right to me.

Q. Did you go any further with the investigation of their books?

A. No, sir. One took the bills and the other the book, and the other the vouchers, and compared them, and we looked at the prices. Captain Horn is in the provision business, and one or two times we thought the prices were high.

Q. After you did that, you did not pursue the matter any further?

A. No, sir.

Q. By Mr. Pleak: What is your business?

A. At the present time I am a newspaper man; my business is practicing medicine.

Q. What is the name of your newspaper?

A. Salem Democrat.

Mr. John Horn, having been duly sworn, testified as follows:

Q. By Mr. Alexander: Where do you reside?

A. I reside in New Albany.

Q. What connection have you with this prison?

A. I am one of the Directors of the prison.

Q. How long since you were appointed?

A. It will be two years the first of next March.

Q. Have you Directors had meetings here investigating this institution, and how often?

A. We generally met most of the time every month, but not always.

Q. About how long between times you did not meet at all?

A. I come up almost every week or every two weeks. I drop in and look around.

Q. About how often do you investigate the accounts of the institution?

A. Every time we have a meeting. You can see in our minute-book the date. We always went over the accounts every time.

Q. When you were here, did you pursue a thorough investigation?

A. As far as the invoices is concerned, we always went through them carefully.

Q. The bills were presented to you by the Clerk with his accounts?

A. Yes, sir.

Q. I will ask, when the Directors met here—when these bills were audited—if these bills were audited as paid when the Directors knew they were not paid?

A. Well, most all bills, when they came before us, and we found them marked paid, we audited them paid. I don't think they were paid when they were before us. I don't know that they were ever marked paid when they came before us.

Q. Did you have any knowledge that some of these bills that were audited as paid were not paid?

A. Not as I know of.

Q. Did you ever have any conversation with the Clerk about the way the institution was managed in which you said you were disgusted at the way things were done?

A. I had several talks with the Clerk. I got very dissatisfied at the way they were paying officers here and guards, and such as the meat bill, I found, had not been paid. I had talk with the Clerk about it, and I told him that the business did not suit me quite, and it was rather loose and so on, and we went and seen the Warden about it and told him he ought to see to it, and he always promised he would.

Q. Did you ever examine the accounts and find out how many outstanding bills were not paid and the amounts?

A. After we looked the bills through, and they were signed by one of the other Directors, I don't think we looked into it.

Q. After finding out that these guards had not been paid, did you ever inquire the reason they were not paid?

A. No, we did not. The only answer we got would be, "That will be all right. I will attend to it."

Q. For what reason was it you did not examine the amount of money he had of every kind belonging to the institution?

A. I don't know whether I could give you any other reason except we had too much confidence in him.

Q. You just went on his promises?

A. Yes, sir.

Q. Did you ever ask about his ability to pay up?

A. We had talks about his paying up, and getting things in better shape. He would say: "Yes, that will be all right."

Q. State if complaints were made to you by outside parties who had accounts that were not paid.

A. Never; no, sir: with the exception of the meat and the guards.

Q. State if when you three Directors were here, did you ever talk over with the Warden about his bills outstanding and not paid, and he promised all three that he would make it all right. •

A. Yes; when we were all here.

Q. Was there ever any proposition made by the other Directors about examining into his ability to pay, and seeing how much money he had on hand?

A. No, sir: nothing of that kind.

Q. I will ask you if, at any one of your meetings, you required of him to furnish you an account of the moneys he had on hand, or the money he had on hand, and of the outstanding bills against the Institution?

A. We did not.

Q. You knew there were quite a number of funds; the convict funds, visitors' funds, money received from the State and on account of contractors. Did you at any one of your meetings require him to furnish a detailed statement of the amount he had received from every source; also, the amount of bills he had paid and what were not paid?

A. Not to my knowledge.

Q. By Mr. Pleak: What did you consider your duty as Board of Directors here?

A. Oh, I think, so far as I know, that we examine into al-

lowances of bills and invoices, and see whether they are correct
with the books of the clerk, to examine the prison, go through
and see whether the food was right, whether prison was carried on right, and where complaints were made by convicts we
investigated them.

Q. By Mr. Alexander: Did you ever inquire for an explanation about how contracts were made by the Warden with
outside parties for furnishing supplies to the Institution, and
whether or not he ever received any rebate by reason of those
supplies being furnished?

A. We never inquired. All we did we looked at the bills
to see whether they were correct with the market prices,
whether they were all low enough, but whether he received a
rebate, I could not tell. We never asked him about rebate.

Q. State if anything of that kind was ever brought to the
knowledge of the Board of Directors.

A. No, sir.

Q. What was said to the Warden when he was re-elected,
by the Directors about his furnishing new bond?

A. That was before my time. I was not Director then,
when he was re-elected. During the first meeting I inquired
about the bond. They said it was the old bond, and the old
bond was good and lawful. The old Directors at that time
thought the bond sufficient. That was all they said about it.

Q. Did you take the advice of anybody as to whether a
bond of that kind would be valid?

A. No, sir.

Q. Just took his statement for it, and the other Directors,
that they thought it to be good?

A. Yes.

Q. You don't know whether they inquired at that time?

A. I could not tell.

Q. What do you know of any corrupt influences that were
used to elect Warden of this prison?

A. Well, I don't know of a thing.

Q. Were there any rumors of that kind?

A. Outside there may be, but I could not take that for
granted. There never was anything said to me or hinted of
the kind.

Q. Was the Warden elected when you came in?

A. Yes, sir. I was going to say: we elected while I am here, a Deputy Warden, the Physician and the Chaplain.

Q. Was there any money consideration offered to the Directors for the purpose of voting for any of these officers?

A. No, sir, not a cent. Even if they offered it, it wouldn't took.

Q. At the times you had your meetings here, if any complaints were made by convicts you heard their statements?

A. Of course. There is no meeting of the year where we have not had those complaints.

Q. You took their statement and then you took the statement of persons connected with the institution?

A. When they made complaints of bad treatment by the guards, the testimony of the guards was always good treatment, and the other side always bad. If any convicts had been worked too hard we always referred them to the physician and inquired into their health.

Q. Did you ever bring any of the contractors before you to find out about these complaints?

A. We went around and asked them, sometimes, what they thought about it. For instance, they would say: "There is a man right alongside of him, not as stout as he is, but he does the same work."

Q. State if you Directors ever said to Captain Howard that you did not think he was conducting the Prison on the right plan—that the management was too loose.

A. Not except what I said about the accounts. Sometimes we told him this had to be fixed. We always got the answer that he would see to it.

Q. State if you ever examined into his rules and regulations to see whether they were reasonable or not.

A. We did. There is much complaint about the food, and so on. When I slipped up here sometimes I never found it different. I thought it good enough for an institution of this kind. I never found any bad meat since I came here. Of course convicts, they complain; you can't please them, whatever you do.

Q. Who makes out your reports to the Governor?

A. We make out the Directors' report; the other is made out by the Warden and the clerk.

Q. State if you ever made any report to him about the manner in which the prison was carried on, as to the money condition of the prison and about bills that were not paid.

A. No, it is not in our report.

Q. Did you make any suggestions as to improvements that were necessary?

A. I believe the report says.

Q. By Mr. Patten: State if that wooden wall was cut down and a brick one put up there would there be a saving in guards?

A. I believe it would be a saving of guards if we had a good wall back there; it ought to be fixed; it is bad the way it is.

Q. Is there not some land here not inclosed belonging to the State?

A. There is some outside.

Q. Do they rent that garden?

A. No, the garden is State property, I think; it is about seven acres, I think.

Q. In what business are you?

A. Groceries, at New Albany.

Q. By Mr. Pleak: Do you ever furnish any supplies to this Institution?

A. No, sir; I have never furnished anything to it, because a Director should not.

Mr. C. H. Walden, having been duly sworn, testified as follows:

Q. By Mr. Patten: What is your connection with the Southern Prison?

A. I am a Superintendent. I have a shoe contract.

Q. Can you furnish the Committee with the amount you have paid to the Warden since the 31st of October?

A. Yes, sir. We have thirty days to pay our bill, and then ten days more. For instance, January bill we should not pay until 10th of March. Some of these bills are anticipated a little. I let them have $500 of November money in October. The payments were made as follows:

October 27, $500 on November account.

November 8, $1,367.93 on September account.

December 6, $1,944.78 on October account.

December 3, $1,995.75 on November account.

January 17, $2,089.63 on December account.

February 10, $2,085.72 on January account.

They get leather from us and shoes, and if there are discrepancies between book and full amount of bill, that can be so explained.

Q. How is it that you pay them in advance?

A. They said they were hard up and wanted some money, and if we could possibly let them have it ahead of time, we let them have it.

Q. Do you remember when the Senate Committee was here?

A. Yes, sir.

Q. Have you any knowledge of where Mr. Howard raised the $7,000 he showed to the Committee?

A. He didn't raise any of it from me.

Q. Have you any knowledge of it? ♦

A. I have no knowledge of myself; no, sir.

Q. By Mr. Alexander: Did you have any talk with him about it?

A. I don't think you have any right to ask me that question. I should prefer not to answer it.

Q. By Mr. Patten : Did you furnish privately any of this money ?

A. I did not.

Q. By Mr. Alexander: Do you know anything about Perin & Gaff, or either one of them, paying to the Warden, or any one, for him, $1,000, during this month ?

A. No; I have heard it intimated on the street.

Adjournment for dinner.

Q. By Mr. Alexander: I will ask whether you know anything about where this money came from that the Warden of the Prison exhibited to the Senate Committee when they were here the other day—$7,000—whether or not you heard Captain Howard say anything as to that; if so, what the conversation was ?

A. I don't think I heard him say anything about it, no more than that he got the money.

Q. Did he say where he got it ?

A. I don't think he did.

Q. Did he say anything about its being his own money or belonging to some one else ?

A. He said the money was there in the safe, if I remember.

Q. State as nearly as you can the conversation you had.

A. I think he told me that he should pull through ; that he

had got the money; had it in the safe there, and enough; the difference his books called for, I think it was $7,000; I am not sure.

Q. State if you had any conversation immediately before Senate Committee came down—as to money part of it.

A. Well that is what I refused to answer this morning. I will say that he asked me to raise him some money. I think my share was $2,000.

Q. Was the money actually due him from you?

A. No, sir; nothing due. It would have been due 10th of April.

Q. Has he asked you for any money since this committee came down?

A. Not a dollar.

Q. Or immediately before the committee came down, and when he knew it was coming?

A. I don't believe I have. I don't think I have been asked to raise any money since the day before the Senate Committee came down, but I may have been. I do not recollect.

Q. Have you had any conversation with him to-day about the committee—about these affairs in the prison.

A. At noon, I think, he asked me about the trouble between me and the committee. He said he understood I was in contempt, and spoke about Perin & Gaff paying him any money last Saturday. I think he wanted to know where I had ever heard it. I believe I told him that I heard it intimated. He wanted to know who told me, would I tell him? I told him no; that I could not afford to tell anybody; that I had heard it. He said, " You think they are on to that, sure ?" I said, "Sure." He asked me, would I tell it? I told him I was going to ask counsel before I answered that question. He wanted to know if I should answer if I had to answer at all. I told him I should tell the truth if I had to answer at all. As I say, I have taken counsel, and my counsel tell me I must answer that question, so this talk really amounts to nothing now. I am ready to answer the question.

Q. The question was whether you knew of $1,000 having been paid to him on last Saturday by Perin & Gaff.

A. I have heard that there was.

Q. Who told you?

A. Samuel H. Perin told me.

Q. I will ask if Mr. Perin said he had furnished him any other money?

A. He is coming before the committee. He can tell you that.

Q. No; he is in Cincinnati.

A. I don't think he furnished the money.

Q. State, if you know, who did furnish this money—the $7,000?

A. I have heard it rumored; I do not know it as a fact; it was understood that Sparks, Lewman and Allen, the Steward, furnished the money.

Q. Did you have any conversation with the Clerk, Deputy Warden or Steward of the Prison in reference to the matter?

A. I have heard them say, I think all of these men except the Clerk, that they had raised the money.

Q. What was the reason they had to raise that money, if they stated?

A. They were short; they had to raise it to make the books balance.

Q. State if you are acquainted with the Directors?

A. Yes, sir.

Q. State when you made your contract and the names of the Directors with whom it was made?

A. I never made any contract.

Q. When was your contract entered into?

A. In 1884.

Q. Who were the Directors then?

A. Dr. Norvell, I think, was one.

Q. Who made that contract?

A. Bryan & Brown Shoe Company.

Q. State how you came to own that contract?

A. The Jeffersonville Boot and Shoe Company bought it from Bryan & Brown Shoe Company.

Q. State if you had any dealings with the Directors or the Warden at the time you made the purchase?

A. No, sir; none whatever.

Q. State if you have any knowledge of any contractors being charged any sum for their contract—any conditions under which they accept it.

A. I believe it is customary to pay something for a contract. I think it is understood that they are to pay something.

Q. Who is the author of that custom?

A. The parties transacting the business.

Q. With whom are these contracts made?

A. With the Directors.

Q. Have you any knowledge of any individual transaction of that kind? If so, state when it was and what company it was with?

A. It is hearsay. The Bryant & Brown Shoe Company paid $4,500, I am told, to the Directors for the contract.

Q. Any other?

A. I don't know of any one else.

Q. What is your source of information in reference to this?

A. The secretary of the company told me.

Q. State what other contracts have been made there lately.

A. The Patten Company is the only company since I have been here. The parties are Columbus people.

Q. Do you know anything about Directors going to Cincinnati, after Perin & Gaff went out—whether you have any knowledge of their advertising for bids?

A. Only in an indirect way. I couldn't even tell you who told me.

Q. I will ask you if task men in the Prison have been granted the right or privilege to labor for themselves?

A. Yes, sir.

Q. By what companies?

A. We have, for one; Perin & Gaff have, also.

Q. What arrangement have you with your men?

A. If a man has done a task, we allow him at the rate of 60 cents a day.

Q. What becomes of that money?

A. We put it into the office. We give a separate check for that.

Q. State about the amount of the monthly earnings outside of your regular quota.

A. Well, it is something like this: We have regular men that we pay any way that do not work on any task. Some men get $5 a month, some $3, some $2, some $1.50.

Q. Have you any knowledge of the purchasing of supplies by the Warden?

A. Only in a general way; that they buy them piecemeal, a little at a time, mostly here in town.

Q. State if any of these supplies are used by the Warden or his deputies?

A. Well, we all see them carrying out stuff every day; that is, bread and potatoes. The Deputy Warden usually boards the guards. Since the change was made in Deputy Warden, the Warden has furnished the guards their meals.

Q. State if that is a frequent occurrence—the taking out of bread and provisions?

A. Daily.

Q. How long has it continued?

A. Since I have been here. A year and a half.

Q. State if you know of the Warden paying the Directors under any circumstances for any privileges or favors? State the source of your information?

A. I could not give you the source of my information. Everybody understands that the Warden has to buy his office. It is understood that they were offered $8,000 the last election for another man besides Captain Howard. That is common report.

Q. State if you know of Captain Howard having to concede anything to retain his position.

A. I do not.

Q. State if you know or have ever heard that he did?

A. I have heard so; common report has it that he had to pay one of the Directors $4,000 or $4,500.

Q. Whose name was connected with that report?

A. Dr. Norvell.

Q. Where did you first hear that report?

A. I have heard it ever since I have been here.

Q. State if there was anything paid that you know of or heard?

A. The election hung fire a long time. The report was, all was going on very lively, and that the Warden, or one of his friends, telegraphed to Norvell that he would give him $4,000, or such a matter, for his corn, and the bid was accepted.

Q. State if you have heard Mr. Jack Howard say anything about it—about having to pay or being solicited to pay?

A. I don't think I have heard him say.

Q. Have you ever heard his book-keeper, or Deputy Warden or Steward, Mr. Allen, say any thing about it?

A. I may have heard Mr. Allen say something to that effect.

Q. What is the number of visitors to the prison during the year?

A. In the fall of the year we have a great many; some days as many as 200, during the exposition at Louisville, for instance.

Q. During the year what is the approximate number?

A. A good many come in that don't pay. There are a great many. Couple of dollars a day would be a fair average. I think I have counted in there 228.

Q. State if, in your opinion, $148 would be a sufficient gate fee a year?

A. I should not suppose it would.

Mr. Walden recalled.

Q. By Mr. Patten: Do you want to make a statement to the Committee?

A. I want to say that I had at one time four men with sore fingers. A great majority of our men have syphilis, and have sore fingers for six or eight weeks at a time. They charge me half price for these men whose work is not worth five cents a day. That is the kind of conniving I have with the officers to beat the State.

Q. You·say a great many of them are afflicted with syphilis?

A. Yes, sir.

Q. Do you know what remedy—what sanitary treatment they have?

A. I could not tell you. They have the chance to see the doctor twice a day if they like.

Q. Are these men suffering right along?

A. Well, if you will come into my shop you can see for yourselves. I have one darkey whose face bunches. We have others that are ready to fall to pieces, but they prefer to work. We have these men, and prisoners rebel against working with them, or drinking out of the same cups. I wish to say that there is no collusion between the employes or the guards, or officials and the contractors, to exact bonus or money for the contractors. I have never been approached on the subject by anyone.

Mr. Richard M. Dennis being duly sworn, testified as follows:

Q. By Mr. Alexander: Where do you reside?

A. In Louisville.

Q. What relation have you with the Southern Prison?

A. I am a contractor in the saddle-tree department.

Q. When did your contract commence?

A. First day of January, 1887. I was sub-contractor, however. I bought out John R. Gathright in July, 1885.

Q. During the month of January or February of this year, did you pay to the Warden any money, and state the amounts?

A. I could tell you exactly the amount if you were at my office. I paid him some money in January. I don't think I have paid him any money this month. I paid him $332.96 in January. I am not sure whether last of January or first of February.

Q. What do you know about any person when obtaining a contract at Prison having to pay a bonus?

A. I don't know a thing of that sort. To the best of my knowledge and belief there has been nothing of the kind.

Q. Within the last week or two, have you been called upon by the Warden to advance anything when it was not really due?

A. No, sir; I have never been called upon to advance any money.

Q. Is there any money due from you to the Warden?

A. I owe him for the present month.

Q. When do you pay that?

A. Well, the custom has been to pay it on the 10th of the month following, i. e., for February we pay on the 10th of March.

Q. How many men do you work?

A. I have thirty. My contract reads thirty convicts with the privilege of fifty. Runs for five years from January 1, 1887.

Q. By Mr. Patten: Do you keep a book showing the over-time of convicts?

A. Yes, sir. I can show you that book to-morrow.

Q. Do you know anything about the prison cash book with the convicts?

A. No, sir.

Q. State how you make return for that over-time, whether it is kept in your account with the Warden or whether it is kept differently.

A. It is paid always separately; I make payment once a month for my different convicts who have done overwork, and write a check for the amount payable to A. J. Howard as Warden. These accounts are all made out distinctly and separately, each one having his proper credit, provided it is entered by the book-keeper. I draw one check for the full amount for that month.

Q. What would be the probable amount of that at the end of a month—take an average month?

A. It won't amount to a great deal: perhaps $20, perhaps $35 or $40.

Q. Do you know whether that is ever credited to the account of the convict?

A. I do not, sir; I can not say; but there is every reason why it should be, of course; I make it out as plain as A B C can be; I keep an account, and know what I have paid each one of them.

Q. Supposing the good time of any of your men was taken from them, how would that affect your labor?

A. I just have so many days' labor; they furnish me so many every day; if there are any sick they charge me up with the men less the sick ones.

Q. If they take a man and punish him you don't pay for him?

A. No, sir; I don't pay for any work or any time except what I get.

Q. How many men do the contractors work?

A. Perin & Gaff had 300 or more, the Shoe Company has 185, I have 30.

Q. What will the labor average?

A. About forty-five cents a day. The Shoe Company, I think, pay sixty cents for some of their men.

Q. I want to ask you if there might be any reform as to contractors in reference to handling your men?

A. There are a great many things that ought to be done. Very hard to tell, the way the prison is built. If it had been more compactly built, and steam power furnished, then all contracts would have been more desirable. Every contractor now has to put in his plant. If it is only for a short time, he don't care much about taking it.

Q. Have you any difficulty in getting along with the officers of the prison?

A. I have had none. Have been treated very cleverly.

The only trouble has been when I first came there. I was amazed at the manner in which the business was done—putting matters off from day to day. There has been a good deal of that. This: "I will see you to-morrow or next day."

Q. What is the course of conduct of the guards toward the contractors there generally?

A. Generally speaking, so far as I am able to find out, the guards try to do their duty between the contractor and the State.

Q. You don't task a man according to his ability or skill?

A. No; I have fixed tasks all alike. You fix a task; some men can do it; others will make fifty cents a day for themselves. I get about twenty per cent. less out of convicts than I would in a free shop.

Frank P. Shields having been duly sworn, testified as follows:

Q. By Mr. Hobson: What connection have you with the Southern Prison?

A. I am cell-house guard.

Q. How long have you been there as guard in the cell-house?

A. I think since about the 1st of October, 1885.

Q. All this time where have you been taking your meals?

A. With the Deputy Warden up to 1st of October, 1886; since that time with the Warden.

Q. How many of the guards are taking their meals with the Warden, or Deputy Warden?

A. I expect from 12 to 14.

Q. How much do you pay him for your board?

A. Now, $4 a week. We used to pay Captain Craig $20 a month.

Q. How many guards have you when you have full set?

A. I think now there is about 30 or 31 guards.

Q. Do you oversee these fellows in solitary confinement?

A. Yes, sir.

Q. About how long do you keep men there in solitary confinement?

A. I never had but few men in solitary confinement.

Q. What offense do you put them there for?

A. We have three men in solitary confinement now that we locked up because they were men that had fights, two of them. We don't let them go to the dining-room for fear of disturbing the other men, and when the other men are eating they rob the cells.

Q. How long do you keep them there?

A. I have got only Brownford, who has been there a week or ten days: the two others have been a little longer.

Q. Do you ever punish them that way for slight offenses?

A. No, sir.

Q. If a man should speak to another one and the guard should see him, can they order him put in this place for that offense?

A. I don't know. I never had a case of that kind. If you catch a man talking in line and you reprimand him, and he persists, we give him what is called the letter A. The letter A takes 20 per cent. of good time off for that month.

Q. If you were satisfied there are men there who have ill will of guards and are tied up for slight offenses, would you consider that pretty severe punishment?

A. That would be owing to the man.

Q. How long is the longest one kept in that kind of position, hung up in this way. [Indicating.]

A. About seven hours. When I have men in punishment I lock them up, tie them up between 7 and 8 o'clock, let them down at 11, tie them up between 12 and 1, and let them down a little before 4.

Q. Do you know of their being confined in this particular cell in cold weather with the windows open?

A. No, sir.

Q. Do they ever complain of being too cold up in that place?

A. No, sir; I never had any man complain to me about it.

Q. Does he stay in there all night without covering and without a bed?

A. It has occurred a few times; yes, sir.

Q. About how often?

A. Well, not very often.

Q. Were they permitted even their coats and caps in that place?

A. No, sir; I never had coats and caps. I tell you what I did do. We had some men I took up there once or twice, and I changed clothes on them, gave them a suit of clothes just like they had. I searched the man. He had concealed a knife and undertook to knife me, and I changed clothes on him.

Q. How often do you see the Chaplain among you and your men?

A. Well, sir, every day or two. Chaplain Cain was very attentive, and this new Chaplain comes in every day or two and talks to my men. He was not there while his wife was sick. With that exception, I don't think he has missed over two days before coming.

Q. If you were told he did not average going in there more than once a month, would you think the party was mistaken?

A. Yes, sir; I would. This new Chaplain is so particular about not infringing on a guard that he has called my attention particularly to it.

Q. By Mr. Pleak: How many men do you suppose he talks to?

A. I never paid any attention; sometimes he will ask me to see one man, sometimes three or four.

Q. Do you attend his services ever of a Sunday?

A. No, sir; I am busy.

Q. By Mr. Hobson: This man up there in solitary confinement as high as 31 days, does the Chaplain come to see him occasionally?

A. I don't know; he goes up in that range. I do not know who he talks to.

Q. This man on whom you took special pity and saw he got a doctor, when you found he had been there for eight months?

A. Well, I don't know how long he had been there.

Q. You saw he needed a doctor. You don't know whether the Chaplain ever seen that man?

A. No, I don't.

Q. You know that these fellows in solitary confinement sometimes have bread and water only?

A. In punishment, if I have a man up there for a day or two, I give him bread and water. A man in solitary confinement gets full rations just as if he went to the table.

Q. How often do you furnish water?

A. They have water furnished them twice a day. Man in solitary confinement gets water three times a day.

Q. What about this man Davis?

A. I have had him sixteen months. He is one of those cranks, takes crazy spells, and you can do nothing with him, and if you lock him up for a day or two he will go out and be a good fellow to work; we never pretend to punish him.

Q. This man Kennedy has been in your charge—how long has he been in confinement in that cell?

A. Well, I think he has been there a month or a little over.

Q. Is it not a fact he has been there since the 1st of January?

A. It might possibly be since the 1st of January.

Q. Did you ever hear of persons staying up there until they froze their feet or hands?

A. No, sir.

Q. You don't think it could occur there?

A. Well, I don't know; if a man stayed up there in real cold weather, through carelessness of guards in making fires, they might, but I never knew a case of that kind.

Q. By Mr. Sinclair: Do you consider Kennedy a bad man?

A. Since he has been in my charge I have not had a bit of trouble with him.

Q. By Mr. Hobson: They all consider it punishment to be confined in their cells, don't they?

A. I have some men that want to go to the cells.

Q. Well, nine out of ten would consider it a punishment?

A. I don't know.

Q. You usually lock them up for some offense, either slight or great?

A. No, sir, we do not. For slight offenses we take off few days' good time.

Q. You confine him, you feed him bread and water, you take and deprive him of the right to correspond with his friends, take away his tobacco and good time for one offense, sometimes?

A. Yes, sometimes.

Q. By Mr. Patten: You have charge of the cell-house?

A. I have. I have certain ranges I lock in. I have three ranges now.

Q. Do you have morning call and make detail.

A. Yes, sir.

Q. Do you keep a morning report of those who are sent to the hospital and those who go to the shop.

A. No, sir. The way we do that, I make my rounds among my men, and every man that wants to go to the hospital falls in line, and we march him up to the hospital, and the doctor examines them; that is after breakfast.

Q. I want to know if there is any account kept of the men. Who reports them to the hospital? Do you make any morning report to the Clerk?

A. We make daily report.

Q. How do you know how many you have for labor?

A. The physician excuses men who are not fit to labor.

Q. How do you make your detail for labor?

A. I have nothing but State men who are not on contract, and old men not able to go on. The other men go from the breakfast table to the shop. I don't have over five or six to go to the hospital.

Q. How does the Warden or Clerk know how many men are at work?

A. We have a little slip, and the guard makes report every evening of how many men he has at work, how many men he has on the roll, how many excused, how many men are first, second or third class. That is handed in to the Clerk in the evening.

Q. Supposing ten more men than his complement went to work and the guard overlooked them, and the foreman of the shop would pay no attention and let them work, how would that knowledge ever be presented to the Clerk?

A. Well, it would be a very poor guard would do that.

Q. Suppose he would collude with the contractor to do that. Could it be detected?

A. I don't know anything about book-keeping.

Q. Where is there any check? How are the Clerk and Warden protected?

A. They can tell in the evening, when we all make a report.

Q. Suppose the guard dishonest and the contractor dishonest, and they would take more men. Is it not possible for them to work an additional number of men without the Clerk ever knowing anything about it?

A. The only way that I should answer that is that the Deputy Warden makes his rounds through the shops. He counts the men and sees if they are there. If the guard misses a man the guard must report it during the day.

Q. You don't make a report?

A. No, sir.

Q. By Mr. Hobson: If there were thirty men due a certain contractor, they could turn him on thirty-five men.

A. Possibly they could if they seen fit.

Q. Have you ever been detailed in the shops?

A. No, sir.

Q. Why is it that man is locked up there all the time instead of being in the hospital, where he could be doctored?

A. You will have to call the Doctor for that. That fellow, I put him up there. He has the pock and he is very offensive. The Doctor goes and sees him. He has never asked to go to the Hospital.

Q. How long has he been in that condition.

A. He come there with it. My recollection is that he come in December, 1885. His name is Delaney Lowrey.

Q. How long has he been in that cell without being relieved?

A. I take him out every few days, awhile.

Q. What is his condition?

A. I have never seen him undressed.

Q. Who attends to that when he goes out to bathe?

A. I take him to the cell house and give him cold and hot water, but I don't stay there and watch him.

Q. Is it not your duty to see that the man cleans himself?

A. Yes, sir.

Q. Are there any running sores?

A. There is many running sores on him.

Q. By Mr. Hobson: How did he come there in that cell?

A. I reported him. He asked me if I would not let him work out in the yard, and I took him out, and he got to running around and wouldn't stay with the wagon, and would go in the shops and talk to the men, and I reported him because he would not mind me.

Patrick McMahon, having been duly sworn, testified as follows:

Q. By Mr. Patten: State whether you were connected with this Institution?

A. Yes, about four years ago, I was night watchman for the contractors, and a little while for the State. I am night watchman for the contractors now.

Q. How long have you lived in Jeffersonville?

A. Since 1869.

Q. Are you acquainted with a butcher over in Louisville, by the name of Duff?

A. No, sir.

Q. Do you know of their bringing beef from across the river?

A. I understood that Mr. Duff was supplying them at the time. I seen the beef wagons come over.

Q. By Mr. Alexander: Did you notice the character of the beef?

A. It appeared to be in quarters.

William T. Royce, having been duly sworn, testified as follows:

Q. By Mr. Patten: Are you connected with this prison?

A. I am in the guard hall.

Q. How long have you lived in Jeffersonville?

A. I have lived here since coming from California, fourteen years.

Q. Are you married?

A. I have a family. I live right back of the prison.

Q. Where do you board?

A. I board at home.

Q. What is your duty as guard?

A. Attending to these gates, letting in employes and visitors.

Q. How long have you been a guard?

A. About fourteen years.

Q. State if you know anything about beef or other provisions being furnished by the prison wagon to any person outside of the Prison proper?

A. No, sir; I do not.

Q. State if it is not a fact that provisions are taken out of this institution to the residence of the Warden, the Deputy Warden and Mr. Allen, the Steward.

A. Well, sir, I don't know whether it goes from the Prison or not. I see bread go out of here. They get their baking done here. Sometimes they bring hams out of the Prison into the Warden's house; nothing else that I know of.

Q. State if you know where the beef supplies come from?

A. I don't know. They come in wagons to the Prison.

Q. Is it not a fact that the wagon stops in front of these residences?

A. I don't know; I am in the guard-room.

Q. Is there not a garden cultivated here for this Prison?

A. Yes, sir; the State cultivates it by convict labor.

Q. Are not the vegetables taken from that garden and taken to these residences?

A. Yes, sir; they take vegetables from that garden, I believe.

Q. How long has that continued?

A. Since I have been in the Prison.

Q. What do'you do when visitors come here?

A. I send for a guard to take the parties through the Prison.

Q. Is there any charge made?

A. I send them to the Clerk to get tickets. The charge is twenty-five cents a ticket. The tickets are taken up by me and put in a box.

Q. State, on your best judgment, how many people visit this institution during the year?

A. I never kept any record of it. I just put the tickets in the box and never think much more about it. Captain Howard passes a good many people free. The Clerk receives the money and takes the tickets out of the box.

Q. By Mr. Alexander: State if there has not been at least 500 to 1,000 visitors in one day during the Louisville Exposition?

A. No, sir.

Q. How much is the largest number that ever visited in one day?

A. I don't think it ever ran up very high. A great number pass free, but there are very few tickets.

Q. What do you mean by a great number? Many?

A. I could not come to make any estimate.

Q. Was there a large number during the year?

A. I suppose it would amount to a considerable number during the year. I don't hardly think it would run up to a thousand during the whole year.

Q. Give us an estimate.

A. I have seen him pass through, without charge, as high as 250 a day. These excursionists come down the river.

J. S. McRay, having been duly sworn, testified as follows:
By Mr. Patten:

Q. You are a guard here?

A. Yes, sir.

Q. How long have you been here?

A. Since the first of January, 1876.

Q. What part of the duty do you perform?

A. When I first came here I was five months in the shops; afterward on night duty four years and two months in the old cell-house.

Q. State whether it was your duty to report the number of men at work.

A. Yes, we always kept a time book. I reported that to the office, of so many men at work, and they kept it on the books also.

Q. What is the manner of treatment of the prisoners? Has that been uniformly fair?

A. There is always a system of reporting men for violations of the rules. In my department, I have tried to manage the men just the same as the Warden would do—make them do right. If a man committed a little offense I would go to him and talk to him, tell him he must do better than that.

Q. Is the tendency of the officers and the guards to improve the condition of the prisoners?

A. I think, in most instances.

Q. Has there been any cruelty or inhuman treatment of the prisoners to your knowledge?

A. Not that I know of.

Q. Who keeps the cells clean?

A. That comes under the various men. The man that has charge of the cell-house now is Mr. Shields.

Q. Is there any bad treatment by guards of convicts for small offenses; that is, is the punishment too severe for the offenses committed?

A. These things do not come under my observation.

Q. State why it is they do not provide better bedding for the prisoners; why they don't keep clean straw. How often do they change that?

A. I know but little about that now, but when I was in there on night duty that devolved on me and my partner, and we always changed bedding.

Q. Is there any reason why this bedding is so filthy and dirty, and is it unusually so?

A. The bedding is generally kept in pretty good order. They have been changing lately. This new contract coming in and the old one going out, they have been moving the laundry away into another department. They have not had the same opportunity to be washing up things in here.

Q. How do they get the straw?

A. They generally get loose straw from the country.

Q. Are any provisions taken out of the prison and carried up to the Warden, Deputy Warden or Steward's residences.

A. There may be some bread taken; it is baked in here.

Q. Is not that a daily occurrence—the taking out of bread and potatoes?

A. Not potatoes, but with bread it may be.

Q. Where do you board?

A. I board with the Warden.

Q. Is it not a fact that all of the provisions taken to the Deputy Warden and Warden's houses are taken out of the prison.

A. That I can not say, anything further than the bread.

Q. Don't you know such a thing does occur—is it not a current rumor?

A. There has been such rumors as that, and I sometimes saw supplies taken out; but I didn't examine them, didn't trouble myself about that.

Q. How many guards generally board at the Warden's or Deputy Warden's?

A. Sometimes ten or twelve, sometimes fifteen or eighteen; the married men generally board themselves at home.

Q. Where do they get their provisions?

A. They don't get them out of here.

Q. Do they keep a garden here raised by convicts?

A. Yes, sir.

Q. Are not the vegetables taken to the Warden or Deputy Warden, whoever boards these guards.

A. I expect they get all they want.

Q. By Mr. Alexander: State if you have received your pay, and how far behind is the pay.

A. I received my pay up to the 1st of November; none since; our pay is due from the 1st of November; they are paid in here; I don't know how; just as the contractors pay in; sometimes at one time, sometimes another. When I wanted money very badly I would go to the Warden, and he would always give it to me.

Q. What do you know about their being behind with the other guards?

A. I suppose they are with some of them; I don't know.

Q. By Mr. Pleak: What do you pay a week for board?

A. Four dollars.

Q. And your salary is—

A. Fifty-five dollars a month. Our board was $4 a week since the 1st of October; previous to that time it was $20 a month.

Q. By Mr. Alexander: How many guards sleep in the prison?

A. Twelve or thirteen. We have these rooms over here. I sleep here.

Mr. James Kennedy, having been duly sworn, testified as follows:

Q. By Mr. Patten: How long have you been guard?

A. Close on to twelve years.

Q. In what department?

A. For the first five years in trip-hammer shop, then transferred to shoe shop, where I am now.

Q. Where do you board?

A. I board at home, right down here.

Q. Do you know at what time the provisions are brought to this institution.

A. No, sir.

Q. Did you see the beef wagons come from Louisville?

A. I think I saw some mornings when we were coming to the shop a beef wagon come in.

Q. Who lives opposite the prison?

A. Some German, I don't know his name. Mr. Knapp, a guard, lives down there.

Q. By Mr. Cruson: How many of the guards are married men?

A. The biggest portion of them are, I guess.

Mr. Isaac Cooper, having been duly sworn, testified as follows:

By Mr. Patten—

Q. You are connected with the prison?

A. I am employed here as night guard; have been for 11 years.

Q. Where do you live?

A. In Jeffersonville.

Q. In what direction from the prison?

A. East.

Q. Do you know of any bread being taken out of this institution to the Warden?

A. Yes, sir.

Q. Is it a daily occurrence?

A. Well, I guess it is, but I am asleep in the day time. I have seen it taken out though.

Q. Is it not a fact that provisions are taken out daily to these officers—the Warden, Deputy Warden and Steward?

A. I tell you, sir, I have seen it.

Q. What time do you come here?

A. I sleep up stairs; I come down stairs sometimes at 12 or 2 o'clock.

Q. State, if you know, where the beef is obtained on the other side of the river?

A. I do not know to my knowledge.

Q. How does it come here?

A. It comes in a wagon, I suppose: I have not seen a pound of beef come into this prison for a year. My understanding was this, that the bread was accounted for in this way. A barrel of flour makes so many loaves of bread, and the bread is accounted for by keeping account of the loaves that is carried out.

Q. Then you think there is no beef, flour, bread, vegetables, anything of that kind, taken to these places without being accounted for?

A. Oh, as for vegetables, they may be taken from the garden in summer. I don't know of anything in the shape of flour going out of here.

Q. What about hams, meat?

A. I never saw anything of that kind.

Q. You come by the Warden's house when you come on duty; did you ever see any provisions shipped in there?

A. I seen provisions come there from up town in grocery wagons.

Q. When the Deputy Warden boarded the guards, is it not

6—PRISON.

a notorious fact that provisions went into that Deputy Warden's house out of this Prison? Is not that the common
understanding of the guards?

A. No, sir.

Q Did not the guards talk about it, that there was so much
charged for their board when it was all taken from the State of
Indiana?

A. No, sir. They did talk about the excessive board they
paid.

Q. Is it not a fact that the best beef was taken and used for
the benefit of the officers of this Institution?

A. I don't know that to be a fact, sir.

Q. Where do you board?

A. I board at the Warden's. I eat supper and breakfast
there.

Q. You say you never saw provisions hauled there by wagons used in this Prison?

A. I saw them with goods that they brought from up town.
Mr. Allen, the Steward, brought them down when he brought
the mail. Mrs. Howard would ask him to bring some things.

Q. Is it not a fact that he has lived the same as the others
—got his supplies out of this Institution?

A. I don't know anything about that, sir.

Q. Why would she say that to Mr. Allen?

A. Because that was the only conveyance she had. She
would know Mr. Allen was going up town for the mail and
send one of the children down, and ask him to stop at somebody's store and get her so and so.

Q. Has the Warden got his own help there to do his er-
rands? Don't he have the convicts do all the work there?

A. The convicts never go anywhere except from here to
his house. He has two girls there.

Q. What are you afraid of? Are you afraid of losing your
position?

A. I am not a d— bit afraid of losing my position; I don't
care if I go out of here to-night.

Mr. Fred Knap having been duly sworn, testified as follows:
Examination by Mr. Patten:

Q. You are a guard here?

A. Yes, sir.

Q. Where do you live?

A. I live down on this street, opposite Prison.

Q. Do you know where they get the Prison beef?

A. No, sir; I do not. All I know is, I see the wagon once in a while. It comes down this street.

Q. Is it not a fact that they get it from across the river from a man by the name of Bloom?

A. I believe so.

Q. Where does Mr. Allen live?

A. He lives up in the city; this is outside of the city.

Q. When do you pass backward and forward to the Prison?

A. I go on in the morning at 6 o'clock, go to dinner about half past twelve, and home in the evening after the bell rings.

Q. How much provision is daily taken out here which goes to the Warden or Deputy Warden?

A. Well, sir, all I know about this: I was here at the gate ten or eleven weeks last fall, and they carried bread out every day. I believe they are still doing it, and once in a while a basket full of potatoes while I was there.

Q. Is it not a fact that these wagons delivered beef, hams and one thing or another to these residences?

A. Not to my knowledge; I never saw it.

Q. What do the guards say about it?

A. I never heard them say it come off the State. I have heard some talk about their paying too much board.

Q. Do you know anything about the beef brought to Prison with the choice parts taken out?

A. No, sir.

Q. Did you see the beef come?

A. I am a very poor judge of meat; I merely seen it and told them to pass the wagon.

Q. Ever seen any bones in it?

A. Oh, yes; certainly. As a general thing, it has been pretty fair meat. All I see of the meat is in the dining room.

Q. How did it appear in the wagon?

A. It was cut up in pieces, 30 to 50 pounds. It didn't come in whole beef.

Q. Do the convicts get any vegetables from the garden?

A. During the summer, tomatoes, parsnips, cabbage, such as that.

Q. By Mr. Alexander: Is the institution owing you for pay?

A. Well, I don't know. It is the custom to keep back two

months. We were paid for October the last pay day. That was some time last month.

Charles Arbegust, having been duly sworn, testified as follows:

Q. By Mr. Patten: Are you connected with the prison?

A. I am, and have been for the last three years.

Q. What is your occupation?

A. That of a gardener. I attend to the garden here.

Q. How is that garden raised?

A. By convict labor, except myself.

Q. You are employed by the State?

A. Yes, sir; I get $55 a month.

Q. State if you raise many vegetables, and what kind?

A. I raise right smart of vegetables; principally green onions, tomatoes, cabbage, lettuce—those kind of vegetables. mostly used in the Prison.

Q. Do you raise any potatoes?

A. No.

Q. Do you raise celery?

A. I raise celery.

Q. About what amount of vegetables do you raise?

A. We raise about all off about ten acres of land. Some of it is very poor land, but while the tomatoes are growing we raise sufficient quantity of them for the Prison. And of cabbage, I have raised three and one-half to four acres of it.

Q. Is it not a fact that the Warden, Deputy Warden and the officials here at the Prison all receive out of your garden all the vegetables that they demand or want.

A. Well, not all; not the officials. The Warden and Deputy Warden do, but there is none others.

Q. But the Warden and Deputy Warden receive all their vegetables from your garden?

A. Oh yes, such as we grow.

Q. How far do you live from in front of the Prison?

A. I live at Captain Howard's—that little brick there. Because of my living there, I have, in addition to the State garden, charge of that green-house.

Q. What becomes of the flowers from the green-house?

A. We decorate the yards. We don't sell any of them.

Q. Do you have an opportunity to know what provisions are delivered at the Warden's or Deputy Warden's?

A. No, sir.

Q. Don't you see the provisions brought in there?

A. I only see what I take in there.

Arthur Brooks, called upon telegraphic request of Hon. C. L. Jewett, having been duly sworn, testified as follows:

Q. By Mr. Alexander: What county did you come from?

A. Wayne County.

Q. When?

A. I came here in 1882; December 30.

Q. What was the charge against you?

A. I shot my family physician for the seduction of my wife.

Q. Give us the circumstances.

A. Well, the sum and substance of it is, I was a stock shipper, away from home a great deal of the time. My brother-in-law lived across the street. He told me about certain things that he had saw which created my suspicion, and one evening I thought I would watch. I had told her that I was going to leave and would not be back until the next day. She attracted my suspicion by her maneuvers, and I got a letter from her which revealed the whole affair. After that I asked her a question and she could not answer, and then she admitted her guilt. I went immediately, got my revolver and shot him.

Q. Killed him?

A. Yes, sir.

Q. What is the term of your sentence?

A. Twenty-one years.

Q. Is anybody interesting himself in your behalf for the purpose of securing your pardon?

A. Mr. Jewett is at the present time. I do not know what he has done.

Q. A petition is out, I suppose?

A. I presume there is one.

Q. What is your wife doing since?

A. She has been living with her own sister until recently. She is now with her niece at Logansport.

Q. Do you correspond with her?

A. She has written to me. I have not received any communication from her for two months.

Q. You may state if you have any arrangement about contract price between yourself and Mr. Jewett, if you will?

A. I told him I would give him $500. I paid him $100 retaining fee, and was to pay $400 when he was successful. I employed Mr. Cain at that time. Mr. Cain did the business through him.

Q. What, if anything, did you pay Mr. Cain?

A. I paid him $50.

Q Who is he?

A. He was the Chaplain. There was a little irregularity. The Chaplain said he had particular influence. He came to me and said he would do a certain amount of work if I would give him $50.

Q. If you would give him $50?

A. Well, he didn't say what he did want in the first place, but he said he was acquinted with quite a number of Representatives and Senators. He always expressed himself as willing to do anything he could in my behalf. I told him one day if he would go ahead and help get a petition and assist me through Mr. Jewett, I would give him $50, and $100 if successful. He said he would do it, and told me the amount of work he would do. I sent for my friend. He came down here and made the payment. I did not hear from Mr. Cain for a good while. Finally, he told me that the nomination was on hand, that they could not do much of anything, but would proceed at once when that was over.

Q. When did you pay him this fee of $50?

A. I think it was in July; my memory is not distinct.

Q. Does he correspond with you about it.

A. No. He came down here just after the election; seemed as if he felt like owing me an apology for not going ahead with the work. He says: "I have just been down to New Albany and saw Mr. Jewett. Mr. Jewett has his arrangements all made and has got everything he wants. We are now waiting for your friend at Richmond. Just as soon as I can write to your friend up there and get a return, I will let you know when we will be at Indianapolis." That was about the 1st of November. I wrote for Mr. Jewett to come, and Mr. Jewett came and he said he did not see him at all that day. He said the only time he saw him was in a crowd one day and simply shook hands with him. I wish to substantiate what I say by Captain Howard. I refer to any writing since the money came, the $150. I wrote to Mr. Cain. Captain Howard did not understand the letter, being as no money came through the office. He called me to the office and wanted an explanation. I told him the money was delivered to Mr. Cain and explained it to him, and he said, I will use his exact language: "If you lose your money, don't you ever say a d—— word to me about it."

Q. What do you know of Mr. Cain getting prisoners to advance money to secure pardons?

A. I understand I am one out of fifty that he has contracted with. Probably fifty or seventy-five. I understand there are at least that much.

Q. Do you know of any of them paying him money?

A. Yes, sir. I know this man, Nelson, in saddle-tree shop. He paid him $50.

Q. What was the average amount they generally paid him?

A. He would take anything. All the way from $5 up.

Q. What do you know about his success in getting pardons?

A. I never knew him to turn his hand over.

Q. What about his communicating with them about their prospects in getting the pardon?

A. I took some pains in finding out. They said they had never known of him as doing anything.

Q. Did Mr. Cain pay the $100 to Mr. Jewett?

A. Yes.

Isaac W. Sanders, having been duly sworn, testified as follows:

Q. By Mr. Patten: Captain, you can state how long you have been in prison, and state how long your term of service is.

A. I was sentenced the 17th of April, 1878, for life. My age is 48 years.

Q. State whether you were a soldier, and what rank you held in the army.

A. 1 was 2d Lieutenant Company F, 10th Ind., nearly four months, and was wounded. Also, Captain Company G, 78th Ind.; Company D, 115th Ind.; Company D, 133d Ind.

Q. Are you drawing a pension?

A. 1 am.

Q. What is the number of your certificate?

A. 198,606.

Q. What amount?

A. $17.50 per month, to commence on the 26th day of February, 1864, and $20 per month from April 3, 1884.

Q. State how much money you have drawn since you have been in this prison.

A. $5,007.25.

Q. What have you done with the money? Can you account for it now?

A. I can not itemize the first part of it. I sent away all up to 18th of last August, except $42.

Q. How did you receive this money from the Government?

A. Through the Warden. He paid it over to me as I needed it.

Q. How much does he owe you now?

A. The way I figure it, $2,300.50.

Q. Did you keep an account all the time with the Warden?

A. I have.

Q. Will you foot up there and see how much you have received from the Warden by your book?

A. All but $2,300.50 of this amount. I paid Mr. Bagot, guard, $67.50.

Q. Did you give orders on the Warden to Mr. Bagot when you wanted to pay Mr. Bagot the $67.

A. Mr. Bagot received my pension checks; I indorsed them and he drew the money. He had charge of the mail.

Q. Did the Warden permit him to open your letters?

A. He was appointed to open all letters. That was his business, to read all mail going in and going out. I left the money in his hands, as I tell you, it would be convenient. He also kept the sutler's store.

Q. Are there any other soldiers drawing pensions in the prison?

A. Yes, as high as ten.

Q. State if he retained any money from others.

A. Not to my knowledge.

Q. You made him your bank?

A. Yes, sir; we are not allowed to handle one cent of money.

Q. Did he account for all the money he had received from you?

A. No, sir.

Q. He received $67.50 of your money; how much did he account for?

A. He accounted for all except $42.50.

Q. What became of Mr. Bagot, where is he?

A. He is not here.

Q. State if the Warden knew anything about Mr. Bagot's transactions with you, taking your checks.

A. I don't know whether he did or not. Captain Huette seen me often about the matter. Captain Huette said it did not make any difference to them about Mr. Bagot handling the money. I told him I had done it for convenience, and I had confidence in Mr. Bagot. He said: "In case of your death, suppose your friends know you draw a pension, they would call here and want an account of all this money. They have no account of it in the office here, and it should come through the office after this." I took his advice.

Q. Who is Captain Huette?

A. He is the Clerk.

Q. State if you paid out any other sums to any person connected with the prison; if so, state to whom and how much.

A. Well, I loaned a guard, Mr. Shields, here now, $25 by consent of the Warden. He was to see I was paid through the office. That was in December last.

Q. What is his name?

A. Frank P. Shields.

Q. Is it paid?

A. It is not paid.

Q. State to whom you paid any other money.

A. I paid some money to Captain Huette for some little supplies—underclothing, handkerchief, socks and such things. Small amount.

Q. To any other person?

A. No; that is all I can think of.

Q. I see an item, "To Chaplain Cain, $10;" what is that?

A. Chaplain Cain did some writing of letters for me, in getting up some papers in regard to petition for pardon before the Governor.

Q. "To Indianapolis Sentinel, $3.65, three months;" does this paper cost that much?

A. I gave Martin, the Librarian, an order for that much. I think he makes a profit for his trouble. He told me 22½ cents on each copy for a month. That included the Sunday paper. I paid former chaplain, Mr. Beherrall, on the 1st of November, $25, and on December 11, 1886, $10. He made three trips to

Indianapolis in the interest of my pardon, and looking after other business of mine. I insisted to put the money upon him. He is a friend of mine. These amounts were all paid with the Warden's consent on my order.

Q. State if the convicts are called upon to contribute money for the purpose of getting up petitions by which they are to secure pardons, or to employ any person?

A. Not that I know of. This dollar you see was given to Billy Taylor to assist him in getting a petition.

Q. State if there are persons here engaged in that kind of work?

A. Not that I know of.

Q. How are these subscriptions started?

A. By the man himself.

Q. By Mr. Alexander: I will ask you whether the Chaplains interested themselves in securing pardons?

A. Not that I know of.

Q. How about Mr. Cain taking an interest in your affairs?

A. I wanted him to do some writing for me in regard to the matter when I was sick.

Q. State if it is not the duty of the Chaplain, if they do not make it their duty, to write for prisoners when they are sick their letters, etc.?

A. Well, I don't know about that.

Q. By Mr. Patton: In reference to this money, when the Warden had it in his hands and you requested him to deposit it in the bank, do you know whether it was deposited in your name or his name?

A. It was deposited in my name.

Q. Have you certificate of deposit?

A. Certainly.

Q. What did you do with that?

A. My certificate was placed in the safe in the office. I signed my name to it and gave it to Captain Howard last week.

Q. Why did you do that?

A. We had a talk about it.

Q. Did you do that for the purpose of his drawing the money?

A. Yes.

Q. You say that you indorsed this certificate for the purpose of his drawing the money out of the bank?

A. Yes, sir.

Q. For what purpose?

A. I do not know.

Q. Did he tell you for what he wanted the money?

A. No, sir.

Q. You permitted him to do that?

A. Yes, sir.

Q. By Mr. Alexander: Do you know what time it was last week that you indorsed this certificate?

A. Friday, February 11.

Q. By Mr. Patten: You have not received that money?

A. No, sir.

Q. How much was that certificate?

A. Twenty-two hundred dollars, even.

Q. Was that certificate correct? Should it not have been $2,300?

A. No, there was some money in the office already. There is really due me $2,300.50, including $25 Mr. Shields owes me.

Q. What did he say to you at the time he wanted to get it?

A. He said he wanted it for a few days. He asked for it the day before. We was talking about other matters, and he said, I want it for a few days.

Q. He did not say anything about the Committee coming?

A. No. I said something about this being the last money I had. He said it was as good as a bank for a few days, but I did't sign it until the next day. Next day, I signed it and gave it to him without saying a word.

Q. Was you afraid not to sign it?

A. Well, of course, I can't tell. I am in very poor health. I say to you I have not been very badly treated, but I don't know if I want to incur his ill will.

Q. I will ask you if under any other circumstances than that which you are in would you have indorsed the certificate?

A. I would not.

Q. State the general management here—whether prisoners are generally mistreated.

A. Persons are not so badly treated now as half a year ago. They have not done any catting for three years; the mode of punishment is solitary confinement and taking good time, hand-cuffing up to the door; but there is not very much of the last.

Q. On what class is it inflicted ?

A. The insubordinates.

Q. What about your food.

A. Our fare is just what you see.

Q. State the condition of your bedding, particularly for keeping clean.

A. Well, the tick—of course you see all that; with the changes and tearing down of walls it is almost impossible for to keep those cell-houses clean. So far as the bed is concerned, whenever there is a call made for a new bed the cell-house guard—Shields is a very attentive man—he sees to that; there could be improvements, of course. I was never in prison before, and don't know what is to be expected.

A. B. Jones, convict, having been duly sworn, testified as follows :

Q. By Mr. Alexander : Where did you come from ?

A. My home is in Lawrence County ; I came from Monroe.

Q. By Mr. Patten : State if you have been employed in the prison as a trusty.

A. Yes, sir.

Q. How long ?

A. Nearly five years.

Statement : Nearly two-thirds of the reports against the prisoners, the complaints of the prisoners, and the punishment of prisoners comes from the shoe-shop, where there is only about 160 men employed, and the cause is very plain to one who is there to see it. Mr. James Kennedy, the head guard there, is an old, experienced, obdurate criminal; he is noted for cruelty, a great lover of gain, a habitual drunkard, and what is here called a Prison Ring Lord. He receives pay from all quarters, and stands ready to commit any manner of crime or cruelty free in the interest of the Prison Ring, or in the interest of contractors for pay. He is warden, guard, foreman, assistant, superintendent and bull dog of the shoe-shop. He has boots and shoes made there for himself and family. He gets a good portion of his fuel there. He often draws on the contractor for lumber ; he has considerable work done in the box-shop and the machine-shop of that institution, and he receives a great many other little presents from there, and pays for all in overtasking and crowding the prisoners in the most brutal manner. He has a son who has been about here the the last

three or four years, sometimes a guard and sometimes a foreman. He is now a foreman in the shoe-shop. He is there
foreman for the contractor to demand the work, and his father
is there a guard to force the work done.

The new cell-house is a perfect chinchbug harbor. The
brick walls of the cells are alive with them every warm spell,
and through the summer it is terrible. The cells smell of them,
the sheets and the blankets are bloody from them, and the
men's skin look horrible from the bites. There was not less
than two hundred men asked and sent requests to Capt. Howard, last summer, to allow them to buy some bug destroyer, but
he refused all; neither would he give it to them nor allow their
friends to give it to them. Two times, through the summer,
he sent some worthless and most worthless prisoners, who lay
around the cell-house, to destroy the bugs, and they done
nothing more than throw a little dust of powder in the cells
which had no more effect than that much water, but it made
an excuse for Capt. Howard to not allow the men to buy the
powder, and that was all it was done for. It is brutal and an
outrage, and a horror only realized by the sufferers.

The rule here is that all money belonging to prisoners must
go into the prison office, and there it goes; and it makes no
difference how much the prisoner needs his money, or how
much his family are suffering for it, nor what the circumstances
and final results may be, it requires a period of time from one
week to three months, and a great deal of trouble for him to
get his money out of the office. I have often known men to
make from ten to fifteen trips to the office, and be months trying to get a little money sent to their distressed families. I am
sure that if you will closely question Mr. Huette, the Prison
Clerk, on the matter, he will substantiate what I have said.

When the new cell-house was built there was gas pipes and
burners put in each cell, but the burners are all taken out, and
now the prisoners are allowed an average of one and a half
very small candles per week through the long winter nights,
and none through the summer; neither are they allowed to
buy them nor their friends allowed to give them candles. What
is it worth to the State for illiterate men to be compelled to let
their books lay on the shelf while sitting in a nest of vermin
and teetotal darkness, while no less than five hundred candles
burn on Capt. Howard's yard fence to light up a political demonstration?

They pretend to give the prisoners pork for dinner four times per week, but the stuff that is given is so fat and strong that not one-fourth of the men eat it, but it is taken off the tables, rendered out, and the lard taken inside. They pretend that they put the lard in hominy for breakfast, but that is false— there is not one-fourth of it goes there. Please closely question Kendrick, their pet cook at the kitchen, and you can catch him lying for them.

The same wagon that delivers the fresh beef here hauls the best of it out again to private parties. Please question Kendrick at the kitchen and Thompson at the shoe-shop concerning the above.

It is terrible the way men suffer here with cold. At the start they took one-half of the heaters out of the new cell-house, and run it so two winters; and then, under false pretense that the house could not be heated with steam, they abandoned the heaters altogether and put in stoves, and the consequences are the men suffer terribly. While they were pretending to warm the house with steam, they kept a stove in one end of the house specially for the guards. It always is a great deal colder in the cells. Now, if the guards with warm underclothes and overcoats on, and generally full of whisky, could not keep warm outside the cells, without a stove to stay by, then how is it with the prisoners? There was not one single Sunday or holiday last winter that I did not lay abed the day through rather than suffer with the cold. It has not been quite so bad during the last two months, since they have become a little scared, but it is brutal yet.

There was a good mechanic, who worked for the State and officers. He was a trusty. His work was principally making bird-cages, making and mending furniture, fine cedar chests, etc. There was a standing order for the contractors to let him have what he called for. He done a great deal of work for George Howard, such as making tables, desks, secretaries, lard coolers, and many other things for his pork-house and store-room. The material was always bought of the contractor and charged to the State, and no other account kept of it. I often bought lumber and hardware of the contractors for George Howard, which was charged to the State, and the amount not known even to George Howard. I built and painted a summer-house for the State in Captain Howard's yard, and Mr. Allen bought 1,000 pounds of white lead, and oil in proportion, to paint the house with, and I used about 100 pounds of the paint, and George Howard hauled the balance back to town and had his store-house painted with it. When asked for the paint and brushes, I hesitated, but George Howard gave me to understand plainly that it was all right with his brother Jack, and he would stand between me and all danger.

There were two prisoners, one a book-keeper for a contractor, the other a mechanic, working for the State and Prison officers. They put their heads together and agreed to keep a private account and see how much the State was losing on certain private parties. So they kept account of all that come plainly under their observation about two and one-half years, until the account reached over $2,500. And then they managed to get the confidence of an honest guard, who had all confidence in one of the Directors, and proposed explaining all to him, which was done by the guard, who asked the Prison Director to go over to a certain shop and receive the written account. But the Director did not have time to go to the shop after the written account, and the guard was forthwith discharged.

Captain Howard's brother, George, built a pork-house in front of the Prison, and a great portion of the lumber and other material was bought of the Prison contractors and charged to the State, and the principal part of the labor was performed by prisoners.

George Howard had two very large and well-finished ice-chests made in one of the contractor's shops, and when he went to settle for them he had the bill changed by counting the hardware and lumber and labor all in as lumber, and the whole charged to the State.

Captain Howard built a house for his sister, and all the finishing lumber was bought of a Prison contractor and charged to the State, and the carpenter work was done by the State carpenters.

In the year 1879 Captain Howard bribed an old life-time prisoner to testify falsely for him, and afterward mistreated the prisoner until he wrote him a letter in plain English (which was seen and read by two other parties) that he had perjured his soul for him, with the promise that he should be well-treated, and now he was being mistreated, and if certain privileges were not allowed him he would turn him over to the law, and Captain Howard, after reading the letter, turned the old man outside to eat in his dining-room. The old man was afterward caught violating the rules and turned in again, and by making another severe threat of exposing corruption he was turned out, and remained out during the remainder of his time. He slept outside and boarded at Captain Howard's house.

[The above sworn statement in writing was delivered to the Committee a few moments previous to their adjournment.]

John R. Tucker having been duly sworn, testified as follows:

Q. By Mr. Alexander: Where do you live?

A. In Jeffersonville.

Q. You were formerly in the penitentiary?

A. Yes, sir.

Q. When were you discharged?

A. Seventh of December last, a year ago.

Q. Do you know of any expenditures there and charged to the State made for political demonstrations?

A. Yes, sir; there were several. Amongst them was a display of fire-works, candles and such things as that in front of Captain Howard's house, and a few before Captain Craig's. We put up quite a fancy work in front of Captain Howard's house—Chinese lanterns and arches. There were nine arches in all and twenty-nine candles on the arch.

Q. Did Captain Howard do that at his own expense?

A. I was ordered out to the work, and I was to make my bill out against the State. The foreman signed the bill O. K., and the Clerk put it on the book.

Q. What would be the probable cost?

A. I don't know what it would cost. The candles were brought from the cell-house. They were candles that were State property; I am satisfied of that. They were kept where State property was. The lumber came from the carpenter-shop. Perin & Gaff furnished that. It was charged up to the State. My orders were to make out the bill against the State. Whenever I did a job of work, the State was charged up with it.

Q. You don't remember the bill of items.

A. There were five of us working on it all day up to 9 at night, when we lit the lights. I was working for Perin & Gaff at that time on contract.

Q. What do you think would be the probable cost?

A. Not less than $75. I don't suppose it would be done

for that. Then there was the time of taking it down next day.

Q. I will ask if you ever heard Captain Howard say how it was paid for?

A. Not much. I never heard anybody only my foreman. I always asked, where is this going?

Q. Any other demonstration that you remember of?

A. Those bells were rigged up last Presidential campaign at the expense of the State. I went over to the paint shop and got my instructions. The bells came from Perin & Gaff. I don't know whether there was any bill made out for them or not. I made the rack for the bells and fixed the frame on the wagon and helped put the bells on.

Q. What do you think was the cost of that?

A. There was three of us working on that all day and about three hundred feet of lumber used. I know that was charged the State. I made out that bill and presented it right there. I think there were three or four bells in a line running across. There must have been fifteen or twenty bells. Different sizes of bells. It made quite a display.

Q. Do you remember the amount of bill charged.

A. I don't. I charged for a full day's time for three of us; there was not less than two hundred feet of lumber. I don't know how much it was worth.

Q. You charged for this labor?

A. Yes, sir; charged the State if I didn't work but one hour. We would charge at the rate of $1.50 a day, while the contractor paid forty-five cents. I was on the contract, but I done nearly all the State carpenter work. I done the repairs around there; made this fencing around Captain Howard's yard.

Q. By Mr. Cruson: Was this illumination the same night as the bells?

A. No, sir. The bells were after the presidential election. This illumination was at the time, I think, of a big speaking here.

Q. By Mr. Alexander: How long were you in prison?

A. I was in prison twenty-six months and one day.

Q. Do you know of any cases of extreme punishment there?

A. I think I got some of it myself which I think I didn't deserve; but there is others punished by guard there for small offenses. There was a fight between two convicts and I attempted to separate them. There were seven or eight of us reported for that (amongst them was Lindsey) without having any chance to see the Warden. We lost our good time eight days. All I tried to do was to separate them. They put me in the cage and chained me up. I have seen Jamison, a guard, knock men down there and kick them when they were not violating the rules at all. I was tied up at cell door, handcuffed with my hands pulled through, and given piece of corn bread and a cup of water. They would stand me on my feet, but I have been shot in the leg, and I was compelled to hang there half of the time with my weight on my arms.

Q. Are the convicts chained up there in cold weather?

A. Oh, yes.

Q. They let them down at night and let them have their coats?

A. Not a single covering.

Q. Did they make beds for them to sleep on?

A. It was simply lumber. Right on the floor was the kind of bed I had.

Q. Do you know of any person being kept longer than one day?

A. I have known men kept there for weeks and weeks. Jim Storey was one.

Q. By Mr. Hobson: What if you had picked up a piece of bread from some other man's plate?

A. They would punish you if it was somebody else's plate. I was reported for taking a smoothing iron from the carpenter shop, and I was not working there at the time. Dickey, a trusty, stole it and took it up to a colored woman, who would give him some money for it and he could get some tobacco. That took eight days good time away from me.

Q. By Mr. Alexander: What do you know about the Deputy Warden and Warden using provisions of the prison at their own houses?

A. It was a regular business. The bread was baked every day. The garden truck was furnished to both places.

Q. What kind of vegetables did the convicts get from the garden?

A. We would get an onion or a tomato.

Q. What kind of meat did you generally get?

A.   As a general thing it was very poor meat. It was so
poor that I once took it to Captain Craig. He had another
piece put on the plate, but it was the same kind. I then informed the captain that the meat was spoiled.

Q.   Did you ever have any roast?

A.   No, I never had a bite of roast, except what Captain
Craig's wife gave to me sometimes. Yes, I got a piece once in
the hospital. We got bacon that was alive with maggots.

Q.   By Mr. Pleak: You saw the beef that was brought in
there?

A.   It was very poor quality of beef.

Q.   How did it come?

A.   Always in quarters and shanks.

Q.   What were your opportunities for seeing this beef frequently?

A.   Just as good as yours would be. There was no restric-
tions on me in regard to that matter.

Q.   By Mr. Alexander: The beds are straw beds?

A.   Yes, sir.

Q.   How often are they filled?

A.   Once a year.

Q.   Did you have any pillows?

A.   No, sir; except what I had furnished by my friends.
That was in '83 I went there. My sister brought my pillow.

Q.   By Mr. Osborn: What about the underclothing?
Were you forced to buy it from the Warden?

A.   I got my underclothing without any trouble from my
sister.

Q.   By Mr. Alexander: Did you have a broom to sweep out
the cells?

A.   I had very small one; had a little hand-broom. When
they wore out they never thought of replacing them.

Q.   How is it if men have to get up at night?

A.   They have little bit of wooden bucket there they carry
out every morning.

Q.   How about the candles?

A.   I don't think we had candles for three weeks, and we
have went there as high as five weeks without a candle. They
were very poor candles; light one of them by 5 o'clock and by
9 your candle would be about burnt up.

Q. How about the books; did you get them whenever you wanted them?

A. No, sir, once every two weeks, and then you had to be mighty good. They would come around and call over names of half a dozen books in a box, and if there is none that suits you you go without.

Q. By Mr. Hobson: Did the Chaplain come here?

A. The Chaplain would come around the shops every few days.

Q. By Mr. Alexander: What about sick men having to go to work?

A. There was a man there had to work, when I know his operations was blood.

Q. Do you know anything about men being overtasked?

A. That was nothing uncommon in the foundry; it was scandalous. I was there a short time, and I had rather be excused and go to that cell-house.

Q. How about the sick being taken to the hospital?

A. I was sick, hemorrhage of the lungs; was in hands of doctor for nine months, and in that time in the hospital not more than one day; hospital patients are treated nicely.

Q. What cell were you in?

A. I was in the old cell-house. A man had better be at his work than locked in the cell. No matter how cold you are, you are never let out to the stove.

Q. Any bed-bugs in the cell?

A. I never seen any thing but bed-bugs. There never was room for anything else.

Q. How about the crazy-house?

A. The crazy-house is alive with rats. It is worse than the hog pen. That is where they put unruly prisoners and call them crazy.

Q. Some of them were crazy?

A. A good many of them went in there and almost came out crazy.

Q. Does the Chaplain preach on Sunday?

A. Yes, sir. They had a Sunday-school for a little while, and then Captain Howard stopped it.

Q. Was it compulsory?

A. That was not compulsory at all.

Q. What was the average attendance at the Sunday-school?

A. Thirty-five. I never missed a Sunday while I was working. Captain Howard stopped that. I don't know just why.

Q. What do you know of any prisoners furnishing any one money to get a pardon for them, the Chaplain for instance?

A. I know Chaplain Cain made a trip to Indianapolis for me, and did not charge me a cent. He was very accommodating.

Q. Did he ever inquire of you whether you had any money?

A. No, sir. He inquired of my family and condition. He remarked to me of what he had done for the boys there, and that there ain't one out of ten ever thanks him for it when they get out.

Q. Do the guards work pretty hard or not?

A. No, sir. The guards in the Prison make men work under contract, and get benefit of it. Jim Kennedy made me work for Boot and Shoe Company, and he would take extra pair of shoes to his children.

Q. Did you make any repairs for Captain Howard?

A. I made repairs while working for Perin & Gaff on his private property that he rented, just back of the prison. I think we worked out there—Gerhardt and I and Dickens. It was two or three days apiece.

Q. Do you remember the dates?

A. No, sir.

Q. How was it charged?

A. That was charged up to the State, I know.

Q. By Mr. Patten: You said a while ago that you was wounded. Do you draw a pension?

A. No, sir; I was in the Confederate army.

Q. Can you read?

A. Yes, sir. I get one book every two weeks, and my sister brought me the Courier-Journal.

Q. Did you take the Jeffersonville Times?

A. Yes, sir. I subscribed for the Jeffersonville Times while I was there.

Q. Are there many copies of that Times taken in there?

A. Yes, sir. More copies of that paper brought in than any other.

Q. Who owns that paper?

A. I have been informed that Captain Howard owned the Times.

Q. Why was that paper taken?

A. They subscribed because they would not allow any other paper in there.

Q. What was the subscription price?

A. I paid seventy cents a month; thirty-five cents for two weeks.

Q. By Mr. Osborn: You spoke of meat being bad. How were your other supplies, such as beans?

A. I have had beans set before me so full of these black bugs I wouldn't eat it.

Q. Do you know about his furnishing such supplies as these that he bought for a low price and charged the State the price of good supplies?

A. I don't know, except from what information I got there, that these things were bought as No. 1. As I said, I showed some meat to Captain Craig, and he told me to show it to the Warden. I did, and Captain Howard told me: "That is good enough for you or any other convict," and the meat was rotten.

Mr. J. B. Merryweather, being first duly sworn, testified as follows:

Q. By Mr. Alexander: Where do you live?

A. In this city.

Q. What is your occupation?

A. Attorney at law.

Q. What connection have you had with the Southern State Prison?

A. I was Warden for four years.

Q. What firm was this that went into bankruptcy owing the prison?

A. The Southwestern Car Company; they had contract with the State to make cars for several years.

Q. They went into bankruptcy, and what was the portion received from the Register in bankruptcy?

A. The State received all the Register allowed. I made a claim as one of the attorneys of the Warden for $27,000, as my recollection now is, but, as attorneys frequently do, I made the account as large as possible. I thought at the time the account was filed that the prison was entitled to about $22,200 or $22,500. They filed offsets and counterclaim. Their offset was that they had furnished materials for repairs of buildings, and their counterclaim, that for two years before Col. Shuler ceased to be Warden he was partially paralyzed and the prison was under less discipline, and the convicts did not do the amount or kind of work that their contract required. Their counterclaim was allowed to some extent by the Register, and the amount he found due to the State was between $7,000 and $8,000. As attorney I paid the witness fees and attorneys' fees. I paid over to Mr. Howard, after paying everything, $6,000 on the 29th of May, 1879. [Check presented and copy herewith attached, marked exhibit "A."]

Q. Have you examined the reports the Warden has made to the State since, that time, and what, if anything, do you know of his having charged himself with having received that amount?

A. At the request, indirectly, of a member of committee, four or five years ago, I made an examination. I found nothing in the clerk's accounts from May, 1879, to that time in reference to money. I find, however, in Captain Howard's report for 1881, in which he says that the amount of money received from car works had been passed or turned in to the brick account: that is the only mention I find.

Q. Did you ever have any conversation with Captain Howard about it?

A. Not until last Saturday. He asked me if I remembered the amount. I said 1 did. He said I certainly could not remember the amount—it was so long ago—and he said, " You can't say whether it was four or six thousand dollars." I then told him I had the check and would produce it to the Committee. I did not show it to Captain Howard.

Q. What do you know, if anything, about the brick account?

A. I know nothing of that, sir, except on examination of this member of Committee four years ago I found the Legislature authorized the manufacture of brick by the convicts, and to the best of my recollection that it fixed the amount that should be expended for the brick.

Q. What was done about the matter before the Committee four years ago?

A. A member of the Committee came to me, my recollection is, four years ago and inquired in reference to it, and I told him, and showed him the check. I had it in my safe. He

said I would be called before the Committee the next day. I
never was called before the Committee, and said nothing more
about it.

Q. About what was the probable number of prisoners during the time you was there?

A. I can't remember. Don't know of any reason why there
should be greater or less number than at present.

Q. How many guards did you have?

A. I had fourteen. I got along pretty well with them. In
summer months I employed two extra guards.

Q. Is there any necessity why there should be more guards
employed now than then?

A. To answer that I should have to go through the shops
and see what is done. If everything is done on the floor, like
a foundry, one guard may guard seventy or eighty men at work.
If the work was setting up barrels, behind which they could
hide, it would require a greater number. It would depend
very greatly upon the business they were at.

Q. By Mr. Patton : Do you know whether the Warden has
ever advertised for contracts for beef and other supplies?

A. I have never seen any.

Q. Where is it purchased?

A. His beef has really been purchased in Louisville all the
time except when ice or flood prevented its being brought over
and then it was bought here. When the Auditing Committee,
of which Colonel Emerson was chairman, were investigating
claims against the prison that had been contracted by Colonel
Shuler, and some contracted by Mr. Howard, Mr. Duff, the
butcher in Louisville, said to me he had contracts for furnishing beef to the hotels and steamboats at Louisville, and that he
furnished the best parts to the hotels and steamers and the fore
quarters and shanks he sent over here to the prison. This conversation took place in the prison.

Q. Have you ever heard of these supplies going to the
Warden's house, or Deputy Warden?

A. Guards at the prison, after they were discharged, have
told me that the same wagon that brought the beef to the
prison took it to the Deputy Warden and the Warden and
Storekeeper's houses.

Mr. Fountain W. Poindexter, being first duly sworn, testified as follows :

Q. By Mr. Patten : Where do you reside ?

A. In Jeffersonville.

Q. What is your business?

A. I am Assistant Cashier Citizens' National Bank.

Q. State if A. J. Howard, Warden of Prison South, keeps his account in your bank.

A. Yes.

Q. How long has he had it there?

A. I could not tell the number of years; probably during all his term of wardenship.

Q. State if he keeps bank account any place else.

A. I do not know of any.

Q. Have you a statement of his account on Friday, 11th of this month ?

A. I have it on Saturday, the 12th, taken from the books on the morning and also the afternoon. The amount he is credited with, morning of February 12, beginning of business, is $7,875.49.

Q. What was it the day before ?

A. I did not draw off balance on day before. I put down balance here, the time the book was balanced ; $65 on February 1, brought down on the book.

Q. State how long it ran at that before he deposited, if you can.

A. I did not make a memorandum of exact dates; I couldn't say without examining.

Q. State if you remember when the Senate Committee was here.

A. My recollection is that they were here last Friday and Saturday, so far as I noticed from newspapers, about the 10th.

Q. State if Mr. Howard had any more than $65 at that time in your bank, on the 10th.

A. I could not give that statement.

Q. When was that difference deposited to his credit?

A. That was on the 11th and the early morning of the 12th.

Q. State if you have any knowledge where that money was obtained, and whose money it was.

A. No, sir; I know the amount was placed to his credit.

Q. Who made that deposit?

A. David M. Allen, or at least part of it. Sometimes he deposited and sometimes the Clerk.

Q. How much was deposited there on Friday and how much on Saturday?

A. My impression is that about $6,500 was deposited early Saturday morning. Balance was to his credit previous to that.

Q. State who Mr. Allen is.

A. I understand he is Steward of the Penitentiary South.

Q. State if you know where that money came from: did you loan it out of your bank?

A. No, sir; I have no knowledge of that.

Q. Did anybody borrow any money from your bank that day or the day before?

A. Not that I know of.

Q. By Mr. Alexander: Anybody else have any deposit there of about that amount of money that was withdrawn, that you know of?

A. No, sir.

Q. By Mr. Patten: Can you state whether checks or cash was deposited?

A. No, sir: I can not. We count everything as cash.

Q. Have you any information in reference to how that money was raised, whether it was Mr. Howard's individual money, or whether or not he raised it among his friends—borrowed it for the purpose of making that deposit and exhibiting it to the Committee?

A. He had no individual account to check on for that amount.

Q. State if you had any conversation with Mr. Sparks, doing business here, in relation to raising this money.

A. No, sir.

Q. With Mr. Lewman?

A. No, sir.

Q. With Mr. Allen?

A. No, sir.

Q. Does Mr. Allen keep an account in your bank?

A. He has no account there. He has had a small account there some time back, but he has no account there now.

Q. Has Mr. Sparks an account at your bank?

A. Nothing beyond firm account. Their firm does business there with us.

Q. Did you have any conversation with Mr. Howard about this money?

A. No, sir, I did not.

Q. Was this a special deposit?

A. No, sir; open account.

Q. How much of that is individual account, and how much as Warden?

A. It is all A. J. Howard's, Warden.

Q. Has he checked out any since then?

A. To-day he checked out $3,333, balance of the account this morning. During the day on February 12, $7,162.27 was checked out.

Q. On Saturday, after he had deposited about $6,500 in the morning?

A. Yes, sir.

Q. Who was the drawer of the check?

A. A. J. Howard, Warden.

Q. To whom.

A. I don't know. I think it was payable to bearer; I don't know. In fact, I was at dinner at the time that was paid out. Cashier Mr. Adams paid it.

Q. When was this $3,000 deposited?

A. One day this week. He made deposit of about $3,000 within the last three or four days. Checked the balance out to-day.

Q. By Mr. Sinclair: Did he check out any yesterday?

A. There may have come in a small check. I do not remember.

Q. What is his balance now?

A. His balance now is practically nothing. Accurately I think it is 12 cents.

Q. By Mr. Patten: State if you have heretofore always honored his checks.

A. We have always honored them if the money was to his credit, but not permitted him to overcheck. I will qualify that. When it is one or two hundred dollars over, we would honor it on the supposition that it was a mistake, but we would notify him immediately.

Q. Does he take up his checks?

A. He took up his checks on February 1.

Q. How did they read?

A. I think most of his checks are pay his office or bearer.

Q. How much has he checked out in any one amount?

A. Seven thousand one hundred and sixty-two dollars, all in one check.

Q. Who got that?

A. I could not say.

Q. Can you furnish the information from your bank? Mr. Adams can tell, can he not?

A. I suppose so.

Mr. Thomas Sparks, being duly sworn, testified as follows:

Q. By Mr. Patten: Where do you reside?

A. In Jeffersonville.

Q. State if you know anything about how that $7,000 was raised by the Warden of State Prison South about 10th, 11th or 12th of February?

A. I know nothing at all about it. I had nothing in any way, shape or form to do with it.

Q. You have no knowledge of how the money was raised?

A. I have not, sir.

Mr. John E. Cole, having been duly sworn, testified as follows:

Lives in Jeffersonville, City Marshal.

Q. By Mr. Patten: What do you know, if anything, in reference to any money being raised here for the use of the Warden at the time the Senate Committee was here, on or about the 10th, 11th or 12th of this month?

A. I don't know anything in regard to the money raising only from outside parties; don't know it personally. Of course, I heard how money was raised. I seen Mr. Huette come to the City Hall, and he inquired in regard to a bill that he claimed the State owed Dorsey. Our City Clerk was acting as City Treasurer at the time. Our City Treasurer is in Thomasville, Ga. I think he made the statement to me that he owed Mr. Dorsey a bill, and he wanted to know whether Mr. Burlingame, City Clerk, was authorized to receive the money. I seen from Mr. Huette's actions that he was considerably worked up, and I took an interest to see what I could do. Well, I learned that the money that was deposited in the bank to balance his account, according to the statement he made to the Senate Committee, was put up by Mr. McCann. He is the man that furnishes the coal to the Prison, and is one of Howard's bondsmen. I heard of several others that had put up the money; on the best of my belief, Mr. Allen. I seen Mr. Allen go to the bank and get a sack of money, and, in conversation with him, he said he was going to pay the guards for four months' wages. I heard conversation between David Allen and Captain Craig. Captain Craig asked him what kind of a Committee he had, and he said : " A s—n of a b——h of a Committee. They had me on the stand for three hours." That was one day last week, either Thursday or Friday evening.

Q. This man, Allen, what is his wealth?

A. I guess between $7,000 and $8,000.

Q. State whether at any time the employes of the Prison, with others, were in the habit of going off on junketing tours, and describe it.

A. It is customary to go on fishing tours twice a year, Captain Craig, Deputy Warden, Dave Allen, steward, Mr. Samuel H. Perin, Mr. Burlingame, myself and others being of the party. The last time we went out, the third time, I went with them. Captain Allen was making his settlement, and I says to him : " Captain, I'm tired sponging off you," or something to that effect; "I want to pay my proportion, I and Mr. Burlingame ; we don't want you to share all this expense," and in reply to it he told me to " Go to h—l; you shan't pay a d——n cent of it," and to the best of my knowledge and belief he said, " The State pays for this," but I would not want to swear that he used the words, " The State pays for this."

Q. Where did he get the supplies?

A. Allen furnished these supplies from Mr. Aiken's grocery ; he buys provisions for the prison from Mr. Aiken.

Q. State what kind of a party it was.

A. We camped out with two tents—a commissary tent and a sleeping department.

Q. State how many blankets you had in the party.

A. Captain Allen said we had a hundred pair of blankets to keep us warm ; that they came from the prison.

Q. How many were there in the party?

A. In going down about eight of us belonged to the fishing party, but we had as many as thirty-six people in camp eating and sleeping.

Q. What was bought from Aiken & Co.?

A. Ham, breakfast bacon, eggs and butter.

Q. What would be the probable expense of the trip?

A. We never stayed less than eight days ; had six or seven gallons good whisky; probable cost would be about $75, including railroad fare.

Q. Who paid the freight bill?

A. It was always paid by Captain Allen; the goods were carted by the prison team to New Albany Air Line Depot and billed from there.

Mr. John Craig, having been duly sworn, testified as follows:

Q. By Mr. Patten : What is your occupation?

A. At present occupied as Superintendent of the Quartermaster's Depot at this place. For eleven years was Deputy Warden Prison South.

Q. State if you know anything about financial transactions that happened two years ago, about the time Mr. Howard was re-elected Warden, and time that visiting committee of the Legislature came down here, in reference to raising $3,000 in behalf of, the Warden?

A. I could not answer what the money was raised for, but I know I, with other gentlemen, indorsed a note for $3,000.

Q. State whether or not you know it was for the purpose of making up the balance of the Warden's account to present before the committee?

A. That I don't know. I know the money was raised for the use of the Warden, but for what purpose I do not know.

Q. Did you have any conversation with him about it?

A. I never had a conversation with him about that. He did not ask me to go on the note. Another gentleman and Mr. Allen, the Steward, presented the note. He said he wanted to raise $3,000 the Warden wanted to use, and he asked me to go on the note.

Q. In connection with that, didn't you know from his statement that the money was for the purpose of balancing his account.

A. I did not know.

Q. What is your impression?

A. My best impression was that was what it was for.

Q. Is that note paid?

A. Not entirely. I think about half has been paid.

Q. Who was the note given to?

A. A little savings loan association here in town.

Q. I will ask if you heard these rumors in reference to your candidacy for Warden of the Prison two years ago, in which you have been charged with offering to Directors something like $8,000 for your election?

A. I never heard it until recently.

Q. State whether or not at that time, or any time subsequent or since, did you have any conversation with the Directors, or ever have any proposition made to them by your knowledge, for the purpose of electing you Warden.

A. No conversation on that subject ever occurred between myself or the Directors.

Q. Did any of your friends communicate between you and them, with your knowledge and consent?

A. No, sir, not with my knowledge and consent. I want to say that I wrote a letter to Dr. Hunter, who resided at Lawrenceburg, and was Director of the Prison at that time. On the eve of the election of the Warden, I wrote to him on the subject of my candidacy for the position of Warden, and I made the distinct and definite proposition to him that I would not be a candidate under any circumstances if Captain Howard was a candidate. From my position there and relation with Captain Howard, I did not feel that I could enter the field against him.

Q. You was acting as Deputy Warden at the time of the last election?

A. Yes, sir.

Q. State why it was there was a delay in that election, if you know.

A. I don't know, sir. I did not know there was a postponement.

Q. I will ask if you was not familiar with the report as to how that election occurred. Was it not common report how it was done?

A. I do not remember it now.

Q. Do you know of any telegrams sent to Dr. Norvell about that time, or before the election?

A. No, sir.

Q. Did you ever hear the report about purchasing about $4,000 worth of corn?

A. I heard that. I think within a year or eight or nine months ago. I heard some guard or somebody connected with the prison repeat it as having come from a young hospital steward named Dr. McFadden.

Q. Why didn't he stay at the prison?

A. Well, I think he was dismissed by the Warden for some dereliction of duty. I know he was not performing his duties in a manner that suited the Warden.

Q. By Mr. Alexander: What do you know about contractors paying bonus to the directors or Warden for the purpose of getting contracts?

A. I know nothing whatever.

Q. By Mr. Osborn: Do you know whether or not the Warden has advertised for bids before letting contracts for supplies?

A. I never saw an advertisement for supplies. I could not say that he has not done so, but I never saw an advertisement published.

Q. By Mr. Alexander: Did he advertise for bids on contracts?

A. Yes, sir, always. That is, I believe always. I have seen those advertisements frequently.

Q. By Mr. Patten: Who does the purchasing of supplies?

A. The Warden. He is presumed to do it, with the assistance of the Clerk?

Q. Does he ever have his book-keeper make out requisition or estimate for provisions?

A. I don't know that he does.

Q. How does he purchase it, in bulk?

A. Yes, sir. Buy a crop of potatoes, two or three hundred barrels of potatoes. Get a contract for meat, five thousand pounds of bulk meat, fifty barrels of beans.

Q. Now, suppose he buy a lot of bulk meat, what facilities have you for taking care of it?

A. They had several thousand pounds together there at one time. Had swinging platform so that the vermin would not reach it, and dry salted it.

Q. By Mr. Hobson: What do they buy corn for?

A. To make bread and hominy.

Q. Where do they grind the corn?

A. In the prison mill.

Q. At the time you was Deputy Warden there, did they bolt their meal in the mill. Where is the meal bolted, or is it bolted at all?

A. If it is bolted at all, it is in the mill, I think.

Q. Do you know whether the meal was bolted?

A. I could not say positively, but think it was.

Q. Have you ever eaten any of the bread?

A. Yes, sir.

Q. Do you think that is bolted meal or not? [Showing sample bread.]

A. I would not call that bolted meal, but it resembles very closely the kind of bread we have there. I would not call that bolted meal for commercial purposes. It is bolted in a manner. The husks are taken out of it.

Q. Do you know how much feed came away from that mill that was fed to the cattle?

A. No, sir, I do not.

Q. How many cattle are kept there?

A. I suppose, altogether, about five or six head at a time. The State don't own any cows. They own some horses and mules.

Q. By Mr. Patten: What do you do with the slops from the prison?

A. The slops were fed to hogs owned by the Warden when there were any hogs at all, and if not, hauled out and wasted.

Q. Where are the slops going now?

A. I don't know, sir. There was a vat made outside to receive slops. They were poured through a funnel in the wall into a vat.

Q. What kind of a place does that create out there—on drainage?

A. It is not wasted in that way. When it is hauled out for waste it is taken out to some place where it will wash. Sometimes we buried the slops.

Q. Could not these slops be utilized in some way?

A. Well, maybe; four years ago, when the Investigating Committee was here, the question was raised about slops, and the Warden and the Board of Directors thought they would offer slops for sale, and they advertised for bids, I think, thirty days, and in the meantime slop was being wasted and buried, and no bid was made. The slops was wasted for three or four months. Finally, the Warden bought some hogs and fed them with it.

Q. By Mr. Hobson: What do they do with the empty barrels?

A. I do not know, sir.

Q. About how many accumulate in a day or week?

A. I suppose it would average about one barrel a day—twenty-five or thirty a month. The business of the prison in the office, and the conducting of its finances and accounts and its supplies, I had nothing to do with. I was simply expected to look after the discipline of the prison, and to see that convicts were properly cared for, that they performed their work, seeing that they behave themselves, and that their relations with contractors were legitimate and all right. I had no business in the prison office, except I was called in for something. Only book I handled was convict register.

Q. You don't think it possible or probable for a man to have been reported sick, and at the same time at work in the shop?

A. There would be no object in reporting him sick. If he was sick, all he had to do was to go to cell-house and lie down.

Q. Could not he have been reported sick and kept in shop working all day at outside work?

A. If he was disposed to be a thief, I suppose he could find his way of doing it, but every foreman in the shop would know all about it. There are daily reports by the guard, giving number of men under guard, number of sick, giving reason why men are not employed, etc.

Q. If he was to tell you he was reported sick and was at work, and asked the Doctor why he was reported sick and said: "I am not sick," and the Doctor said: "Well, you know why," would you believe it as the truth?

A. No, sir.

Q. By Mr. Patten: Is the Deputy Warden required to make a report in the morning of the number of sick and the men detailed for labor?

A. The report of the sick is made from the hospital every morning and every evening. The guard in each shop renders report on printed form of number of men employed on contract, and if all are not there, he explains the cause. That is made directly to the Clerk.

Q. Suppose the guard was derelict in his duty and failed to do that or make false report, how is it tested?

A. I don't know that there is any systematic test made of it, but I say it would be impossible to do a thing like that with any convict.

Q. Supposing guard makes report of so many men, suppose some man is off duty and he wants to shield him, how would you know that all your men were not on duty unless you compared the number of men at work and the number in the hospital?

A. The Warden and Clerk are supposed to do this. They get these statements.

Q. What becomes of the reserves, the old, those unable to work—how is that accounted for?

A. That is accounted for on the report similar to what the shop guards make, but made out specially for cell house guard.

By Mr. Hobson:

Q. It seems to me you keep these men in the cell too much. What is the reason for that?

A. Well, I am not prepared to say it is actually necessary, but I think lounging around the shops is detrimental to good discipline. There was a time, after the failure of the Southwestern Car Company, when all convicts were idle for several months; then we herded them in the shops with several guards over them.

Q. State how many guards are necessary and have been kept.

A. I can't say exactly, but my recollection is that the average during the number of years that I was there would be about 30.

Q. State how these guards are selected.

A. I do not know; I know they come on the recommendation of Directors and others, but I do not know what influences are used. The Warden has the power of appointment.

Q. Did you ever hear that the guards claimed that they were charged a fee or bonus for their place?

A. Never heard an intimation of that sort.

Q. If there was such a thing, I suppose that would be made known when the guard was discharged.

A. Yes, sir; if it was a violation of contract I presume the guard would squeal.

Mr. L. F. Cain, having been duly sworn, testified as follows:

Q. By Mr. Patten: State what relation you have sustained to this Prison.

A. I was moral instructor from 14th of July, 1883, to 15th of September, 1886.

Q. In our investigation we find that a convict named Sanders has paid you $10 in money?

A. Yes, sir.

Q. Will you state just what that was for?

A. I don't remember just exactly the date Mr. Sanders paid me $10. I did some work as attorney—made a trip, I believe, to his home to fix up some pension papers, etc. I was Hospital Steward and Physician for six months, and during the time I was here I was admitted to practice at the bar. The money was not paid to me at the time I was Chaplain.

Q. State if you were here two years ago, when the Warden was re-elected, and if you have any knowledge of any corrupt means being used in that connection.

A. Well, I saw no money change hands in that election of Warden. I have no positive knowledge of money changing hands.

Q. You have no knowledge of your own, have you any knowledge of any corrupt transaction?

A. I have heard it, of course, currently reported that money was used. The nearest positive information is such as I have given to a member of this Committee. I believe that Dr. Hunter told me himself.

Q. Who was Dr. Hunter?

A. He was at that time one of the Prison Directors.

Q. Now state what he said to you.

A. I think he said it to me himself. I am not sure whether he said it or whether I got it second-hand, but I am of the impression that he told me himself, that a gentleman came into his office and asked him if he would cast his vote for a gentleman for Warden for the consideration of $3,500. He told him he was not that kind of man; if that was his business, he could leave his office. He offered the money in behalf of Captain Craig, who was then Deputy Warden.

Q. Have you any knowledge of corrupt practices or attempted practices between Mr. Howard and the Directors?

A. None, save rumor.

Q. What kind of a rumor do you mean?

A. Just simply a general report.

Q. By Mr. Alexander : State if you did not write a book on the prison and its management when you went out.

A. I have a book now, pretty nearly ready for the press, in regard to the State Prison, concerning the treatment of convicts, and the weak places in the law, as I regard it, as to the moral instructor, the way he is hampered.

Q. By Mr. Patten : Do you remember a man by the name of Goodwin ?

A. Yes, sir.

Q. When was he discharged ?

A. Pretty soon after Governor Gray's administration began.

Q. Did you do anything in getting his discharge ?

A. He asked me to work for him. I told him I would if I could do any good. He gave me $15. I made three trips for him to Indianapolis, and went to New Castle and disposed of his property for him. His wife paid me the $15. Goodwin said when he received his pardon he would settle with me. It cost me $65 in expenses. I worked persistently to receive the pardon for him because I thought he needed it. When he was pardoned I supposed he would come and see me. As he did not, I went down to his residence, but found nobody at home at Mr. Goodwin's, and learned that he had gone West.

Q. At what time was that ?

A. Part of the work was done just before Governor Porter left.

Q. You did the work while you was Chaplain ?

A. Yes, sir; I did.

Q. State if that was a custom of yours, while you were Chaplain, to be using your influence in getting pardons ?

A. I have assisted a good many. I got up briefs of the cases, and would also get petitions, where the convicts were not able to employ an attorney. In all, I did not receive more than $50 to $65 from them.

Q. Did you usually receive pay for it ?

A. Sometimes I did, and sometimes I did not. In the majority of cases they were not able to pay, and that was the reason I assisted them.

Q. State if you did not intend to publish your book right away after you left the prison.

A. Yes, sir.

Q. Why didn't you do it ?

A. I intended at that time to get the book out before the election in pamphlet form, but the pressure of the work when I went to Salem was such I could not possibly get it out before the election. Then I decided to get it out in book form. That was the only reason of that, sir.

Q. State whether or not you ever received or were offered a consideration from the authorities here not to publish that book?

A. Never offered a cent. It never was mentioned to me by any officer of this Institution, except the physician, and, he and I are good friends. He said he wanted a copy of the book, and I asked him for his photograph to be put in the book. I received a present a short time after I left here, as was always the custom with Chaplains. I received a gold watch, charm and cane.

Q. By Mr. Alexander: This book had reference to the moral instructor being hampered by the Warden or Directors; in what respect?

A. No, he is hampered by the State laws. The Chaplain, under the law, can not enter this institution without permission from the Warden. He has no more right than a convict has. I had no right to visit a shop without special permission from the Warden. I offered to teach in school if they would furnish the men, but there is no place where school could be taught. I never had the men or received the men in a place where I could teach. I have no authority to go into a cell. It simply puts us here to do what the Warden and Directors allow, and nothing else.

Q. By Mr. Pleak: Is there any rule of the Prison preventing that?

A. The rule of the Prison has always been that the Chaplain could have access to the hospital and go around the Prison ground, but there never was a rule which permitted the Chaplain to take a man away from his work. The ruling is always that the Chaplain had no right to enter the institution. Of course, I came in and out pretty much as I pleased.

Q. You were never prevented from going in?

A. No, sir. The law provides that the Chaplain shall buy new books. I purchased about two hundred and twenty-five dollars' worth of books out of the library fund while I was here. I was here three years and three months.

Q. Did that exhaust the fund?

A. Oh no; we had during the Exposition 500 or 600 visitors a day.

Q. By Mr. Sinclair: Strike an average as to the number of paying visitors.

A. The year I was here was during the Exposition. I would put that in at ten a day. I put that as a minimum rough guess.

Q. Can you suggest any needed improvements?

A. I have preached in that chapel when the men were actually in a suffering condition because of the cold in the winter time. I have preached in the summer time when I have had as high as five men prostrated by the heat because of the iron roof.

George W. Miller, being duly sworn, testified as follows :

Q. By Mr. Patten : Where do you reside?

A. Martinsville.

Q. How long have you resided there?

A. Since '73.

Q. Where did you reside before that time.

A. I was born and raised in Hendricks County.

Q. State if you are acquainted with Mr. A. J. Howard, Warden of the Penitentiary South?

A. Yes, sir.

Q. How long have you known him?

A. I first met Mr. Howard on the 8th day or March, 1883.

Q. Under what circumstances ?

A. I was sentenced to the Southern Prison to serve a term for three years; was there twenty-eight months.

Q. What was the charge against you ?

A. Procuring an abortion. I was afterward pardoned out by the Governor.

Q. State if you was in and about the office at the Prison ?

A. Yes, sir; I had a great deal of liberty there.

Q. State if you remember the time when the Warden was re-elected?

A. Yes, quite well.

Q. Do you know anything about that transaction?

A. As I heard it from an officer of the Prison. Although I had a great deal of privilege, personally the things I am going to relate I don't know, except as I got them from one of the officers of the institution. He told me one night; the Hospital Steward, by name, John C. McFadden. He came there after the death of Dr. Jesse McClure and took his place. One night he took me out after office hours and after the lights were blown out, and all should have been abed. I was chief nurse in the sick ward of the Hospital Department, and this McFadden took me out into his room, unlocked the doors contrary to rules, and took me out there. He had a jug of whisky out there and we got a little exhilerated. One of the night guards came up and we had a general good time; had a lunch and smoke.

Q. Was that outside of the prison?

A. It was in a room adjoining the hospital department, not outside of the walls. While we were drinking out there, this question came up, not only once, but a number of times, as to how Howard was re-elected, and McFadden and I talked about how it happened, how a man of his reputation ever happened to be re-elected. McFadden says: "I can tell you all about it. I was a ward of Senator William Raum, of Evansville, and was in his office a great deal, studied medicine there, graduated there, and once while in his office Raum told me to take a dispatch over to the telegraph office and send it, and that dipatch read: 'Dr. H. H. Norvell, Bloomfield, Greene County: Sir— If you have concluded to let me have your corn draw on me for four thousand dollars.' He said the dispatch came immediately back and he carried it to Senator Raum. 'I have drawn on you this day for four thousand dollars. H. B. Norvell, Bloomfield, Greene County.' He said that Billy Raum threw up his hands and laughed, and said: 'Jack Howard is the next Warden of the Southern Penitentiary.' I asked him what 'corn' meant? He said: 'Never an ear of corn passed between them. He was the man who negotiated for Norvell's vote. He stood between Norvell and Howard, and he negotiated with this man Norvell for Howard for the next Warden.'" I told Howard about it afterward myself, while I was a prisoner, and Howard told me "everything was fair in war and politics."

Q. Proceed with your statement.

A. Howard told me that W. D. H. Hunter, another one of the Directors, was a stubborn fellow, and had been offered a round sum to vote against him, and that he would not vote against him nor for him, from the fact that he had a man of his own he wanted to elect as Warden, and Hunter would not do anything only stick to his own man, and he was mad because Norvell changed from his own man to Howard, and that Dr. Hunter left in disgust, would not stay any longer. Major Finney, a Republican, was a Director at that time, and I think went out that day or the next. At any rate, he remained Director just long enough to vote for Howard, and it is currently reported that he received $2,000 for his vote.

Q. Who reported it?

A. There was a convict in the penitentiary by the name of Ignatius Buchanan, to whom the guards gave every confidence—told him more, probably, than they would tell any free man in the town; in fact, he knew everything that passed on the outside, and Buchanan told me that the guards gave him to understand that Finney got $2,000 for his vote, and it was generally conceded. Oh, well, the question as to the Warden's sell was never questioned; it was conceded there by everybody.

Q. What do you mean by saying the report was never questioned?

A. We always wanted to know what authority there was for a report first, and Buchanan said a guard told him, and that settled it.

Q. How did the guard come into the confidence with these men?

A. We did not know anything about that, but there was Mr. Cooper and Mr. Jamison; in fact, there was not a guard but he was specially confidential with Buchanan; they brought him a bottle of whisky nearly every day, contrary to rules.

Q. Do you remember the day on which this election took place?

A. No, I could not give the day.

Q. Did you ever hear any other report only this from McFadden as to the telegrams between Senator Raum and Norvell?

A. That is all.

Q. Was that the first time you heard it?

A. Yes, sir; that was the first rumor.

Q. And from McFadden's statement it became a rumor?

A. Yes, sir. I asked Howard about it, and he said: "Everything was fair in war and politics." He said it in a jocular manner.

Q. Don't you suppose if it was a fact that he did that, and you spoke to him about it, that he would have been surprised and wonder how you knew it?

A. He asked me how I knew it. I told him it came from McFadden. I said: "If McFadden is telling these things about you, why do you retain him?" He said, "Oh, well, sometimes on account of favors we keep men here we do not care to keep, but we rather have to keep them."

Q. Did he deny it?

A. In a jocular manner only. He told me, "All was fair in war and politics."

Q. Did you ever hear him seriously deny the charge?

A. Oh, no, sir. What I say is all he said about it.

Q. State whether or not that was after the Legislative Investigating Committee went down there two years ago.

A. The conversation I had with Captain Howard was after the Committee was there.

Q. Then the Committee had been there before McFadden made this statement?

A. Yes, sir.

Q. Do you know personally of any money transactions between the Directors and the Warden?

A. No, sir.

Q. You say Mr. Finney voted for Mr. Howard?

A. Yes, sir.

Q. Did you ever have any talk with Mr. Finney?

A. Oh, frequently.

Q. Did you ever have any talk with him in reference to why he voted for Mr. Howard?

A. Oh, no, not at all.

Q. You don't know from any other source or any other persons any facts in connection with this bribery?

A. I will leave that point open, if you please. I will state at this present time I do not remember of any other.

Q. Are there any other facts in connection with the prison you desire to state to the Committee?

A. As to the Chaplain, L. F. Cain, I wish to say the law of the prison, as I understand it, is that all the funds received from visitors passing through there—25 cents each—were to go to building up the library of the prison, and all money found on the person of a prisoner, after he was once inside of the prison, was taken for the same purpose, and that was considerable from the trinkets they sold to visitors or money they otherwise received. No prisoner was allowed to have money on his person. The number of visitors who pass through there in one year I have made a rough estimate of. I think it would be sure to be at least that much, an average of five persons a day. I have seen one hundred pass through there in one day. And in all the two years I was there, there never was but one batch of books bought, and they were principally medical books, because the Chaplain was then studying medicine, and he bought these books for himself and charged them up to the fund. He bought Gray's Anatomy. The kind of book he bought, the way it was bound—it was a poorly bound book—probably cost $3.50. It was charged at $6 or $6.50 to the State, and when I told him it was rather extravagant for that book, he said, "Oh, well, that is customary," and laughed over it. Judging from that, if the other books cost that way, they were rather costly books. But the books he got that time would probably have cost $40 or $50. That was right under my supervision. I would often go through the library, and in all the time I was there that was all the books ever bought. Evidently there must have been $300 a year library fund, but what went with it I could not tell.

Q. By Mr. Alexander: State if you know anything about Chaplain Cain was dealing in procuring pardons.

A. Chaplain Cain told George W. Fort, of Hancock County, that for $50 he would procure a pardon for him.

Q. Did you hear him state it?

A. I did.

Q. State whether or not that was at the time he was serving as Chaplain.

A. Yes, sir, it was. At one time he called the lifetime men together and told them if they would donate him so much money, some considerable amount, I do not remember just now, that he would go before the Legislature and he would procure the passage of a bill making fifteen years a lifetime sentence; and they gave him the money, and he went to Indianapolis, and when he came back he laughed and said, if they don't get their bill through he would get his bill through to raise his salary from $800 to $1,400.

Q. Do you know of any person who would know something about the amount of money he received?

A. I did know, exactly; fifty or one hundred dollars, maybe more. I know they donated pretty liberally.

Q. Did he claim to be a lawyer?

. A. Oh, yes, sir, but he claimed his influence was sufficient.

Q. State what intercourse the convicts might have with the outside.

A. The guards would carry in whisky, not all of them, but some of them would carry in whisky or anything else that the men wanted to buy. The foremen of the contractors would do the same thing in the shops. The trusties, of course, carried in anything they might get hold of on the outside.

Q. What do you know, if anything, about any of the guards and officials being drunk?

A. I have seen Captain Howard drunk fifty times, I guess. Not down helplessly drunk, but intoxicated. I have seen Dr. McFadden, the Hospital Steward, so drunk I put him to bed, I don't know how many times. I have seen Mr. Jamison, the guard, when he was drunk.

Q. What do you know of any one having charge of the keys and getting drunk, so that a person not intoxicated could take the keys?

A. Well, Dr. McFadden would get drunk, and I have taken his keys and carried them in my pocket for half a night. I could have let out all the persons in the hospital department—attendants, sick men and all, without his knowing anything at all about it. I would put him to bed.

Q. Was that a frequent occurrence?

A. Oh! yes, sir.

Q. By Mr. Patten: Was this traffic going on with the knowledge of any of the officers—this carrying in of whisky, etc.?

A. Yes, sir; I told Captain Howard. It was my duty to report to him how the Hospital was conducted.

Q. How were you treated?

A. I never received a cross word from anybody except Dr. McFadden. Dr. Graham, I wish to say as we go along, was a noble man. I seemed to be preferred. Dr. Graham would call on me when he wanted any consultation rather than McFadden, and it made him mad. He tried to get up a scheme to get me into trouble. He tried to get Buchanan to take one dollar's worth of opium down and tell a man named Lowrey that I had sent it to him, but old Buchanan was too honest. They found it out, and he said that McFadden gave it to him himself. It was against the rules to give out opium to persons unless it was a dose for prescription. In giving it in bulk that way, of course, it would ruin me. For all that, McFadden stayed until he got to drinking and carousing about so that Captain Howard quietly asked him to resign.

Q. By Mr. Alexander: What about this man Buchanan having his money taken from him?

A. Buchanan, Ignatius Buchanan, frequently told me as to having deposited the amount when he went there, and his trunk and gold watch. He told me what pages the entry was made and about Shuler stealing his money, and about Captain Howard covering up the steal and having the pages torn out, and so on. He had some $3,300 in all.

Q. He was a convict?

A. Yes, sir; life-time; he went from here.

Q. What leaves did he say were torn out?

A. The entries 66, 69 and 71 of the cash book.

Q. By Mr. Patten: Who cut the leaves out?

A. I could not say that. Captain Huette went to look it up for him on the sly, to see what was coming to him. It seems Huette was rather friendly to Buchanan, and he found it out.

Q. Did Mr. Huette ever say anything about it?

A. Clerk Huette told me that the leaf was cut out, and he could not tell about it.

Q. By Mr. Alexander: What about this man O'Neil who was found dead?

A. I can only refer to prisoners who told me. They were acquainted with that transaction. James Hudson, Oram Batey and Ignatius Buchanan, all life-time men, and McDonald Cheek. They said he was found dead, hung up to the door, after begging to be let down.

Q. Did they say what he was punished for?

A. Some infraction of the rules; I don't remember what the specific charge was.

Q. Do you know anything about a man being burnt in the furnace?

A. I heard that frequently. That happened before I came there.

Q. What about the convict who is said to have escaped to Tennessee?

A. That is the man who should have been burnt in the furnace. It was reported that he had escaped to Tennessee, when, in reality, as report has it from these prisoners I have named, that a guard struck him too hard and killed him, and they could not bury the body for fear of investigation, and took it to the furnace, made the firemen and others leave. When they came back they found evidence of a man having been burnt in the furnace. Then it was reported he went away. Pieces would come out in the Tennessee papers about the man having been heard from, and so on, and Captain Howard is said to have sent detectives down there.

Q. Do you know these engine men?

A. These men I speak of could tell you that; I can not.

Q. By Mr. Patten: What evidence did they discover there, as reported, of his being consumed in the furnace?

A. It came to me that they came there, and thought it a very singular transaction that they should have them go away at such a time; it was in the night time, and when they came back they looked to see what they might have been doing, and they found evidence of the remains of a person who had been burnt in the furnace.

Q. How long did they stay away?

A. A couple of hours.

Q. Is there any other matter you wish to speak of?

A. You ask the same men I have named about Dave Allen taking a lot of fluters, fluting irons, worth $1.50 or $2 apiece. Everybody knows as well as they can know anything that never came out positively that David M. Allen stole a couple of hundred or so of them, and was about to get caught in the transaction, and he had a life-time convict, a nigger named Dave Roper, from Terre Haute, say that he stole them, with the promise that he should have a nice position. Roper did go out and swear that he stole those irons, and since that time he has been head cook. He has the privilege of tinkering about and doing as he pleases. He makes toothpicks and such trinkets, and sells them, and does as he pleases. He is a fractious fellow, and if it were anybody else would be in trouble frequently, but they do not punish him at all. Captain Allen has him in charge, and it is generally conceded that is the reason of it—that Captain Allen would get him a pardon, and give him a good position while he was there.

Q. By Mr. Sinclair: Is there any other transaction that you know of?

A. Do you know anything in regard to the dairy? I worked at the house, that is, superintended out there and the cows—now I won't say positively they were State cows—they were reported to be. The convicts took charge of them and milked them, 7 or 8 very fine cows, and they carried the milk to the house, and the milk that was taken up to the hospital, about probably a gallon a day, was charged up to the State, and the Directors allowed pay for it right along, and they sold milk, I guess to twenty families around there, and appropriated the money, put it down in their pockets. I thought it was a little singular that it should be so was the reason I took notice of it.

Omer T. Bailey, having been duly sworn, testified as follows:

Q. By Mr. Alexander: How long have you been here?

A. Nearly sixteen years.

Q. What county did you come from?

A. Well, my home is in Dearborn; I came from Franklin.

Q. For what crime?

A. I was implicated with being accessory to a murder committed there. Sent here for life.

Q. What place did you have when you first came here?

A. I was on the contract in the pattern shop.

Q. Did you ever have charge of an engine?

A. Yes, sir; I had charge of one while it remained in the wash house. Have one now there.

Q. I would like to call your attention to a particular time, I don't know just when it was, and ask you about the circumstances, when some man was punished for some offense, and died and never was buried—do you know what became of that man?

A. You ask too many questions in one; I will tell you as far as I know in regard to that matter. There was a man here that underwent punishment, and was found dead, hanging at his door; I think his body was buried out here in the graveyard; I don't know that he was, but he was carried out.

Q. What was his name?

A. His name was O'Neil.

Q. You say he was taken out of the prison yard and buried?

A. Well, that was the supposition—that he went out. We see the coffins go out, and the ambulance, and suppose the man went out.

Q. You say he was found dead—did you see him?

A. I seen him after he was dead; I didn't see him when he was hanging at the door. He had been there all night from the day before.

Q. Do you remember the season of the year—know what kind of weather there was?

A. No, sir. I could not give you any definite answer, because it has been sometime ago.

Q. Do you know whether he was white or not?

A. I don't know. I think he was white.

Q. Did you ever have any conversation with the officials about it?

A. There was a general talk throughout the prison about the man. The rumor was the Doctor had excused the man from duty, and sent him as an excused man to the cell-house. He was ordered to be strung up by the officials, and found. dead in the morning at breakfast time.

Q. Did they lay him out?

A. They took him to what is called the dead-room, attached to the Hospital.

Q. What was the rumor here about the prison as to whether he was ever buried or burnt?

A. There was a great many versions about it. Some were under the impression the majority that die here their bodies go to the Louisville Medical College. At one time for a long while I had charge of the graveyard out there. I used to make coffins. I heard rumors of that kind, and when there was to be a burial I would go and strew sticks and straws about the grave, and would go out the next morning, and in a good many cases they had been disturbed. I have seen men sitting right up on the railroad track. They were piping off the place we were planting the man, in order to have their chance of getting the body.

Q. At any time you had charge of the furnace or engine, state whether or not you ever found any bones, or what you thought were the remains of a human being.

A. Well, there was a circumstance took place here that was previous to the O'Neil business. There was a man by the uame of Goddard. He was a twenty-one-year man. He was a man pretty high strung, and so considered, still, a good fellow to get along with. I remember he got the displeasure of some of the guards in some way or other, and, after his day's work was done, they took him to punish him. He was a man, I guess, had never been in the habit of letting any one do that without making resistance, and he resisted, and they got away with him. I know this much about it. It was out and was common talk that Goddard was dead, and everybody knew he was enjoying good health when he was taken from his day's work the evening before. I couldn't tell all the rumors that was afloat. Some rumors was out that he resisted, wouldn't allow them to punish him and they hit him a little too hard and killed him. That was the common rumor. I don't know personally that this happened. At that time I was running the laundry, and the boilers that supplied the steam was in the center of the yard down there. I went down there in order to get the fireman to put on more steam. He was out of sorts, and cut me off very short. He said, " I would like to know how a man is going to furnish steam when the boiler is burnt," and called my attention. I looked in the boiler, and there was a blister, or cat-face, on the boiler the shape of my hand, what is called a cat-face. There must have been ex-traordinary heat there and had burnt it. I said, " What caused it?" He said, "Ain't them bones there enough to satisfy you?" and " that's burnt meat." They did that, and he mentioned certain parties.

Q. Whom did he mention?

A. He mentioned D. M. Allen for one, Mr. Kennedy, the guard, for another; and Arthur Hilliard, who was guard here, had charge of the cell-house at that time. I took a stick and punched the bones and meat around, and looked at them. I said that was curious kind of meat. He said : " I should think so. There is where Goddard went in, right there, and was burnt in the furnace. They came here last night, and me and my partner was told to go away and keep away for two hours until they accomplished their object."

Q. Who told them to go away?

A. Mr. Allen had that place in charge, and told these men—the fireman and assistant—to go off about the kitchen

and stay there, and said: " When we want you we will call
for you," and these men come there and found the bones.

Q. The rumor was Goddard died very suddenly; was it
said that he was buried?

A. The rumor has it Goddard died very sudden, but there
was no such thing as the body being taken out.

Q. When a man is buried, is there anything put about his
head, giving his name?

A. There is a small board; they generally put their name
on them.

Q. This is before you had charge of the grave-yard?

A. No; that was after they had taken it off my hands. I
had more duties to perform than I could possibly do.

Q. Have you ever made an examination to see whether
Goddard's grave was marked in the grave-yard?

A. I never seen it, although I have been there a hundred
times since.

Q. These bones you saw, what kind of bones were they?

A. They looked to me nothing like animal bones. Looked
to me more like bones from man's wrist and ankle bones.

Q. By Mr. Patten: Did you see any skull?

A. There was a kind of cinder there, big as a half-gallon
measure; peculiar kind of substance.

Q. By Mr. Alexander: Did you see anything that looked
like the back bones?

A. I couldn't tell you. I am not so well acquainted with
the anatomy of a man, but the bones looked different from
animal, and, from the remark he made, I scrutinized them a
little closer than what I would otherwise.

Q. What was his name?

A. This man was named Robert Roscoe.

Q. What became of him?

A. He is down here now near Bedford. He is a farmer.
Put in ten years' sentence here.

Q. Did you ever hear Allen, or anybody else with Allen,
have a conversation about this man, as to what became of him?

A. No, sir. He never had much use for me—Mr. Allen.
I don't know for what reason. I suppose he thought I was a
little too close an observer for him.

Q. Did these guards mention it?

A. No, sir; none of them ever mentioned it. Of course,

there was general rumors and talk about it among the men, but nothing that I could give you accurately.

Q. How long ago was it that this happened—when you saw these bones in there?

A. It was somewhere, I believe, in '75 or '76.

Q. Who was the Warden at that time?

A. Captain Howard.

Q. Who were the Directors?

A. I believe Captain John Kirk, from Madison, was one; I am not able to tell you.

Q. Did you ever have any talk with these guards or officials of the Prison in regard to the matter; when you thought their suspicions were raised, did you ever mention the case?

A. I have told certain guards myself what I knew about it. I believe I told Mr. Cox about it and the Clerk.

Q. Did Allen ever say anything about it to you?

A. No, sir; but he appeared to have a spite at me, and he would vent it out at me; sheared me of many privileges I had. I couldn't approach him, no matter on what subject, and when sent to him direct by the Warden, but he would give me the bluff and cut me short, and do everything he could to browbeat and intimidate me. I have heard him say, "There is Bailey; it wouldn't do to let him know anything;" that was the way he would get it off.

Q. What are the names of these persons who know about this matter?

A. There is Henry Caldwell, colored, had more or less to do around the furnace, and is said to have seen the man put right in; he is a river man, and is at Evansville, or Henderson, Ky.; and there was another man, Paul Abel, now at Seymour; he was the assistant fireman.

Q. Where are these guards?

A. Kennedy is employed in the shoeshop; Hilliard lives here in Jeffersonville.

Q. State what time it was in the morning when you went there and found these bones.

A. Right after breakfast time. They should have done this thing in the evening after the day's work, and after the prisoners had all gone to the cells.

Q. By Mr. Patten: Who was the guard that had charge of him?

A. I think Mr. Kennedy was in charge of the trip-hammer shop, and think he was the man had charge of him.

Q. Do you know who the parties were that beat him?

A. These parties I have mentioned—Captain Allen, Mr. Hilliard and Kennedy. They was in the habit; they come in here, and if they choose to punish a man they went right ahead and done it.

Q. Without any authority?

A. Yes, sir.

Q. Can you fix the date this happened?

A. No, sir.

Q. By Mr. Sinclair: Do you know it was during Howard's administration?

A. Yes, sir; because he came in with a vengeance and made everything hop from the start. There has been some terrible work done here, if it ever could be got out. All unnecessary, too.

Q. By Mr. Alexander: When did you come here?

A. I came here the 24th day of May, 1871.

Q. How long after you came was it that this happened?

A. Well, it was three or four years; four years probably.

Q. What season of the year?

A. It was along in the fall, if I am not mistaken.

Q. Do you know of any other transactions like that having occurred?

A. There has been a good deal of brutality shown here; this case, in particular, of O'Neil's. Why, I spoke with the Doctor, and he told me himself it was a terrible thing and rested on his mind day and night that the thing had occurred. They claimed that Dr. Sherrod didn't excuse the man, and Dr. Sherrod went up to the Hospital and fetched down his books and showed where he ordered the man to his cell and excused him from labor during that day, and there was quite a wrangle as to who was right and who was wrong. He claimed they had punished the man without his orders, when he had excused him.

Q. Do you know where O'Neil came from?

A. I do not, sir. He was here for larceny.

Q. What was Goddard here for?

A. He was here for manslaughter.

Q. How long after you came in was it when this O'Neil case happened?

A. This O'Neil business happened six or seven years ago; six, I believe. I tell you they strung him up there. The House Committee arrived here the afternoon the thing occurred, and in the morning he was dead, when they first entered the Prison to examine into things.

· Q. By Mr. Patten: Had they any knowledge of his death?

A. I believe they held a post-mortem on him. Dr. Edmunds, he was a physician that was on the Legislative Committee. I believe their verdict was that the man died from congestion. I suppose it would cause congestion to any man to be hung up by the wrists and stop the circulation.

Q. How long was he hung up?

A. I couldn't tell you how long he was up before they let him down. They usually go to the Hospital in the morning and the doctor passes on them, whether he excuses them or sends them to the shops; then in the afternoon, too, at 8 o'clock. I don't know whether they hung him up in the morning or afternoon. He was hung up there all night until the next morning.

Q. By Mr. Patten: Can you give the names of the guards who had charge of him?

A. This man, Arthur Hilliard, had charge of the cell house, and he had a colored man with him when he opened the door and the fellow was hanging there. This man was in the habit of going with him. He is dead now, took very peculiar disease, no physician could understand it, and he passed away very mysteriously, and the man looked like he was able to stand anything.

Q. By Mr. Alexander: Did you see Mr. O'Neil after he was dead?

A. Yes, sir, I seen him.

Q. Did you make any examination?

A. No, sir, just went in and seen him.

Q. Did you examine his wrists?

A. No, sir, I did not.

Q. By Mr. Patten: What did Captain Howard say to the Committee?

A. Well, I don't know as I could tell you anything about that at all. He always makes light of everything. Always tries to impress upon the Committees' minds they need not believe a word anybody tells them. That has always been his object—laughing and ridiculing any statement man makes before anybody, and it was almost as much as a man's life was worth heretofore for him to make any statement at all to visitors of any kind.

Q. Was any severe catting done?

A. This man, Mungo, we all knew he received a terrible castigation, because the blows could be heard in the yard. Some say he was hit 50, others 100, and others counted 120 stokes. He was put in the Hospital and died. McDonald Cheek called my attention to it.

Q. By Mr. Patten: How long ago was that?

A. Somewhere in the neighborhood of the time this O'Neil matter happened.

Q. State if the severity of the punishment has been abated.

A. Yes, within the last two or three years, it was nothing to what it was before that.

Q. Who were the Directors at the time that occurred?

A. I am not able to state. I saw his back and the flesh was sloughing off from the effects of the cat. You could see the blue streaks where the cat went. Chaplain Boring, of Paoli, Orange County, knows about it. I went to him and said: "Are you a humane man." He said: "Yes, I am, and I can't stand this thing much longer. I am going to put a stop to it, if there is a law in the land." This man, I think, has a a memorandum of all the dates of things that occurred here.

Q. Where did Mungo come from?

A. He was a transient man, supposed to be a half-breed Cherokee Indian. I know men connected here who do not want to express themselves. It is almost like signing a death-warrant.

Q. Do you know of any men being punished after they had made any statement?

A. They would trump up some trifling excuse and punish him.

Q. Were you ever threatened if you said anything?

A. No, sir, but it was always considered if a man would come before the Committee they would get even with him.

James M. Hudson, convict, having been duly sworn, testified as follows:

Q. By Mr. Alexander: How long have you been here?

A. Going on 21 years.

Q. Where did you come from?

A. From Vanderburgh County, Evansville.

Q. What are you here for?

A. Murder.

Q. Did you know a man who was here in the prison by the name of Goddard?

A. I was not personally acquainted with him, but the name is familiar.

Q. Can you call him to mind now?

A. No, sir, I don't know that I can.

Q. What became of that man?

A. I think he died here, some of them state.

Q. How long ago was that?

A. Ten or eleven years.

Q. Do you remember about a man that was burnt up in the furnace?

A. It was said, but I don't know this to be a fact, it was said that there was a man burnt here in the furnace about that time.

Q. Was it only rumor that you know?

A. Just rumor, I don't know anything of the facts.

Q. Do you know anything about a man named O'Neil, who died here?

A. Yes, I helped carry him to the hospital. I was working in the cell house. It was in May, six years ago, maybe longer, maybe eight years ago. I was at work in this old cell house, and Mr. Jack Hilliard was the day guard in there, and he says, "Hudson, come here; there is a man up here I want you to carry to the hospital." I went up on the range, and said, "Where is he?" He said, "In there," and I stepped in. The man was in there, dead, and I gathered hold of him with three or four others, and we carried him to the hospital. The man was dead.

Q. Was he strung up?

A. I can't say. He had been strung up. I think he was strung up then, but they had him down before I got there. I took hold of the man after we got to the hospital; took hold of his arm, and his arm was stiff, just about in that shape [indicating bent elbows, hands toward shoulder]. This part of the arm worked [above the elbow] and this [below the elbow] was stiff.

Q. What did you notice about the wrists?

A. I did not notice anything about that, but I knew the man had been hung up there.

Q. What did the guard say about it?

A. They said that he had been sick that night. They did not talk much about the matter with me. That was about the talk.

Q. Did you hear Mr. Jack Howard say anything about it?

A. No, sir.

Q. How long had he been tied up there?

A. I think he had been up there eight to ten or fifteen days; I am not certain.

Q. What makes you think he had been there that long?

A. There had been talk among the prisoners that such and such a man had been up there so long.

Q. Do you know what became of him; did they bury him?

A. I can not tell you anything about that, sir; the last I saw of him was in the hospital.

Q. What was his given name?

A. I don't know, sir.

Q. What do you know about his being sick before being put up there?

A. I don't know anything particular about it. The man appeared to be complaining. I had been up to the hospital several mornings and saw him there.

Q. Just before this?

A. Yes, sir, I think so.

Q. Was the man a large, robust man, or not?

A. He appeared to be a tolerably stout, hearty man, medium size, I think.

Q. Do you know what kind of work he was at?

A. No, sir, I do not, but it appears to me like he was at work in some machine shop. It runs in my mind that way.

Q. Did you ever hear the Warden say anything about it?

A. No; a man talks very little to the Warden.

Q. Did you ever have any talk with the physician, Dr. Sherrod?

A. Yes, sir; I was quite friendly with him. Sherrod said he died with heart disease.

Q. Did you say anything to Dr. Sherrod about his being strung up?

A. He knew he was strung up. He was physician at that time. Sherrod was mad about it. Sherrod didn't think the man was in anyways dangerous. He had examined him the day before. He didn't think the man was as bad as that.

Q. Did the doctor say he thought the man died with heart disease?

A. That was what he told me. I said, "Doctor, your man is dead up there." He said, "Yes, I am sorry about it." I said, "What was the matter with him?" He said, "Heart disease, I reckon."

Q. Did he appear like he believed it was heart disease?

A. He just spoke it the way I tell you.

Q. Have you anything to state to the Committee?

A. Well, I don't know that I know of anything in particular.

Q. Do you know of men having been punished for testifying before legislative committees?

A. I expect there has been a good many punished the last twenty years; not that alone, but they would pick up something to get them on. I don't want anything to do with them.

Q. Do they work you hard?

A. They work me too hard. That brought on this paralysis. I have to wear a heavy steel truss—hurt when I was molding. I was charring coal in the sun was what brought the paralysis on.

Q. How long since you had paralysis?

A. About twelve years, I think.

Q. But they give you a good deal of privilege now?

A. I don't know as they do. I have been here so long they don't pay as much attention to me as when I first came.

Q. This negro you speak of, was there any rumor that he had been killed?

A. That was my understanding. There was a rumor among the prisoners that the nigger had been killed and burnt up.

Q. And the negro disappeared?

A. He was not here.

Q. You remember of having seen him?

A. Yes, sir.

Q. Was he stout, able-bodied?

A. He was pretty stout.

Q. About how long was it until you missed him?

A. Well, I was talking about it a day or two after he was gone. There was some fellow says, "Do you know what became of that nigger?" I said, "No." He said, "I guess they killed him and burnt him up in the furnace." I said, "I guess not." He says, "That is what they say."

Q. When a man dies naturally in the hospital, don't they usually have a coffin and shroud, and·is it not generally known to all the prisoners?

A. Certainly; I worked in the hospital there about three years when Sherrod was there; they make old box coffins, cheap old things, put a shroud on them, dig a grave and bury them. I believe every man that died while I was there was buried, but how long he stayed out there, I don't know.

Q. It is known by other prisoners that that man had died?

A. Yes, sir.

Q. And the men know he is buried?

A. The men up there do, but not the men in the shops.

Q. They generally take them out in the ambulance?

A. Yes, sir; spring wagon.

Q. You never heard anybody say they saw the negro go out?

A. No, sir; I don't know that they did.

McDonald Cheek, having been duly sworn, testified as follows:

Q. By Mr. Alexander: How long have you been here?

A. Fifteen years next May—28th of May.

Q. Were you acquainted with a man in here named O'Neil?

A. Yes, sir.

Q. Did you know him very well?

A. I only knew him from my connection with him in the hospital. But before I testify, I want to make an explanation. I have had considerable trouble here; not any vicious trouble, but I have been hounded around, and I have consumption, and it is mighty hard with me. I don't want to say anything, but I will state the facts about this, as I am under oath. Six years ago the Committee was down here; Mr. Rolker was one and Mr. Wilson was chairman, and they told me I should have protection and should not be mistreated, and they had hardly got away from the prison until I was fired out of the hospital;

I was nurse there, and just kept after me, and I was locked up.
Dr. Sherrod ordered me out of the lock-up cell, but they paid
no attention to it until he saw Captain Howard and told him,
" You take that man's life in your own hands by keeping him
in that cell." They turned me out then, and first one and the
other picked on me, and I concluded, under these circumstances, I would not say anything about it. Now, you can
question me, and I will tell the truth.

Q. You knew O'Neil tolerably well?

A. I was nurse in the hospital. They brought him in there
once, sick. I could see he had the asthma, and the doctor
asked me to see to him. That was his practice; I had made
medicine considerable of a study. He could not breathe. I
prepared some medicine and gave it to him, and the next
morning the doctor examined him, and left him in the hospital
for two days; then they sent him back to the shop, and he
stayed there in the shop, I think, about a week, until they
brought him back to the hospital again and left him for that
night, and he was booked out again the next morning. He
stayed in the shop two days, complained, and was fetched to
the hospital. Dr. Sherrod told me to examine him. I examined him, and he asked me if I thought he was able to work.
I said, " Doctor, I don't find anything the matter with his
lung. He complains of smothering in the throat and breast.
I sounded his lung, and couldn't see anything wrong in the
lungs. He did not seem to flinch." Sent him back to the
shop to work. He failed to do the task, was reported, taken
up and locked up, and it was four days from that time until he
came to the hospital again and begged to be put at some other
work, and said, " For God's sak, take me down out of that cell."
The doctor said, " Take you down out of what cell." He said,
" They had me locked up ever since I was up here." The Doctor jumped on his feet and said: " By God, I will see who
runs this institution. I ordered you to a change of work."
Mr. Hilliard, a guard, came up and said: " I will see to it,
Doctor," but instead of changing the work, they took and
hung him up again, and they had him hung there in the cell,
sick as he was, all night. In the morning I went around attending to my duties, and just as the Doctor came in, one of
the runners, I believe a man named Reef, came in and said:
" Doctor, they want you over at the cell-house." The Doctor

told me : "You go in there and attend to the sick until I get back." I went in, and he came back and, said : "Hell's to pay now. There is a man dead over there in the cell-house." As I was cleaning up the ward they came carrying the man in the dead-room. His face was set. His hands set in that position [indicating as if resting on elbows].. Around the wrists you could see where the hand-cuffs had been set; mortification was all around. Dr. Sherrod said to me: " You leave that man just as he is ; don't you touch him." "All right," I said. Dr. Jesse McClure was Hospital Steward here. He was at Louisville, attending medical college, and I was attending to the sick while he was gone. He stayed at night and Dr. Sherrod in the day time. They sent me for him, and me and him went into the dead-room to see O'Neil, and after he stood there and looked at him, he said : " What is your orders ?" I said Dr. Sherrod said, "Leave him just as he is until the Coroner came." He went away and came back and said : "Get some water right quick and wash this man, and put a shroud on him." I says to him : " Dr. Sherrod said for me not to touch this man until the Coroner held an inquest on him." He said : "Never mind what Dr. Sherrod said ; do as I tell you." Then I went in and got the water, washed him, took off his clothes and put a shroud on him. Then Colonel Kegwin and Dr. Beckwith, of Jefferson-ville, friends of Dr. Sherrod, came up here to visit Dr. Sher-rod, and they went into the dispensary, and the Doctor and they had a little lunch there. Dr. Jesse McClure called me, and says: "You go in the dispensary and get the post-mortem case, but don't say anything to Dr. Sherrod or let any one see you get it." I said: " What should I do if the Doctor asks me about it." He said : " Just make some excuse for getting it." I went in and stepped behind the door, said " Excuse me, Doctor," picked up the post-mortem case, and walked out. Dr. Jesse said to me : "Take it into the dead-room." I took it, went to his room, knocked on the door and said : "Doctor, that post-mortem is in there." I then seen Dr. Foutz and Dr. Sidney McClure sitting in Dr. Jesse's room ; then they went into the dead-room and locked the door. I met another man, by the name of Cary Tony, four-year man, United States man, and I said to him : " Does Dr. Sherrod know they are holding a post-mortem examination on that man ?" He said: "No, and

I should tell him." I said I had orders not to tell him, and says, "You can tell him if you want to." He went and told, Dr. Sherrod. The old Doctor came out tearing; he went to the dead-room door to open it and it was locked, and they would not let him in. He hallooed, but they would not pay any attention to that. He asked, "Who is in there?" but still they would not let him in. He commenced pulling up his sleeves and come up to me and said, "What in the hell does this mean?" I said I did not know what it meant. He knocked again, said he would kick the door down; still they would not let him in. He come back to Tony and me and said, "Will you men stand by me," and then commenced kicking and said, "I will go in there if I have to kick the door down," and then they let him it. He said: "Gentlemen, this is a nice way to treat me. I am physician of this Institution. By what right do you come and hold a post-mortem on this body." They had some words then, of course, but they shut the door and we did not hear any more. After he came out, they went away, but just about the time they were going, they called me in to sew up the corpse. Instead of opening the breast and laying it back, they just cut the whole breast out. They had taken the lungs and heart out; the lungs lay in one wooden bucket and the heart in another, and they took his liver out. I asked Dr. Jesse whether I should put the liver, heart and lungs in, and he said "No." Just then the Investigating Committee came in; some of them rushed in the room and broke right out again, and would not stay in there. I went away to wash my hands, and, to tell the truth, I kept dodging the Committee; I wanted to keep out of the way. They came into the kitchen, and wanted to question me. I kept telling them I had nothing to say. You go in there and see for yourselves. Some went in and some did not. They stayed in there about an hour before they left. After they left, I found they left everything as it was and spread the shroud over the corpse as it was, and the Coroner came up and I showed him in, and he come in and seen the blood on the sheet. He said: "Who held a post mortem on this man?" I says: "Dr. Foutz, Dr. Sidney McClure and Dr. Jesse?" He said: "H'm, h'm! who authorized them to hold that post mortem?" I said: "I don't know anything about it, sir; you will have to ask them?" He said: "H'm, hold a post mortem," raised up the cover and

walked away. That is all he did. Seen the little blood on the
sheet and did not look any further. He could have seen, of
course, the heart, lungs and liver in the buckets. Captain Howard came up there, and Captain Craig, and commenced talking, but I did not pay much attention. Congestion of the
lungs or congestion of the heart was, I believe, the decision
they rendered. After the Committee was here, Dr. Jesse
told me that they were going to send for Governor
Porter, and had orders not to bury him. Dr. Sherrod and I
went there after the Committee left, and the Doctor says: "By
God, they are trying to put this off on me; make me shoulder
the blame for killing this man." He says to me: "You know
I had nothing to do with it, and the books will show it." I am
a pretty good hand at examining lungs, and says I: "Doctor,
show me where there is any ulcers on them lungs." He looked
over them. He said: "Congestion there, h— and d—, there
is no more ulcers on his lungs than there is on a bull's horns."
I picked up the heart then and turned it over, and said: "Doctor, that looks like a pretty healthy heart; it is a little fatty."
The Doctor looked at it. Says I: "Don't look like there was
much congestion there." "Congestion, hell," he says, "by
God, having man hung up to the door until he dies and then
call it congestion." That was all he said, and walked out. I
saw he was angry. That night Dr. Jesse told me to get the
post-mortem case. I got it, and I and him went in the dead-
room. He took the lungs and told me to cut them. They were
lying in the water. I asked him what he wanted, and he said
he wanted to dissect them. He wanted to see where them
ulcers was. I handed him the knife, and he says: "No, you
take and cut them." He said: "I don't want to touch them.
I want you to do it." I said: "Why?" He said: "Well,
you are a better hand than I am. If anything is said about it,
they can't blame me and they can't hurt you." So I went to
work cutting the lungs up; cut them all to pieces, hundred
pieces or more, took them up piece by piece and looked at the
ventricle tube and the cells of them and everything. "Dr.
Jesse," says I to him, "I don't see many ulcers on there." Says
he: "No, sir; they don't seem to show up very much," and he
made the remark: "Mack; if you had as good a pair of lungs as
them you would be satisfied, wouldn't you?" I told him: "Yes,
sir; I would." Then we took the heart and dissected it, and just

the same as we did with the lungs, I cut it all to pieces, and then took the liver and done it also just the same; I cut it all to pieces; all by orders of Dr. Jesse McClure; and we stayed in there until half past 11 o'clock at night. The next morning Mr. Hinton told me he was on the Committee; that they intended to take the body to Indianapolis; and Dr. Jesse came in and said to me: "They talk of taking this corpse to Indianapolis. If they do, there will be a big kick about these lungs, liver and heart." "Well," I said, "what shall I do with them? Shall I put the pieces in or shall I leave them out?" He said: "Gosh! it would not do to send the corpse up there without any liver, lungs or heart." He said: "Put them in." I picked up all the pieces and put them in the coffin. I opened the breast stitches, and shoved them in there, and put the stitches back again. The Committee here stayed until next day, and the water was up so high they concluded to let it go, and we buried him in the Prison graveyard.

Q. Did any of the Committee look at him and inquire why his arms were in this way [indicating]?

A. I pulled his arms down. I laid them across his breast and tied them so I could keep them down. They were set, but you can take the arms of any man that is dead and put them in any position you want. No, sir; I had taken the arms down and had his shroud on before the Coroner came in.

Q. Was anything said to you about hurrying?

A. I had orders in the first for to hurry up and dress him when Dr. Jesse first came in. He wanted to get him dressed to keep from showing the position he was in. When he came in he was just as Roach cut him down. Mr. Hilliard said: "When I let him down in the cell, he just fell back and died." Roach said he was dead before they took him down. I don't know where Roach lives. I think he came from this county. Mr. Hilliard lives in town.

Q. You say Jack Howard—when that man was up there dead—had a quarrel?

A. Dr. Sherrod and Hilliard was the men that had the words. Hilliard said to him: "If he was not able to be punished it was his fault for letting them go." Dr. Sherrod said: "By God, it was not his fault. They never consulted him."

Q. What do you know about a man named Goddard that died in this prison, or whether you know he died?

A. He was a white man. Well, I could not say very much about this. I don't know. I would not swear anything concerning Goddard.

Q. It was reported that a negro died?

A. Mungo was the man that was catted.

Q. Tell us about it.

A. Mungo had some trouble over there about a file in the shop; some difficulty about a file being missing. The foreman went around and asked for the file, and no one knew where it was. Some of the prisoners told him Mungo had it, but he said he did not have it, and had no use for it. They searched around his berth, and found he had the file; and they had some difficulty, he and the foreman. Anyhow, he was taken to the office. I believe Captain Harveston was guard. I think he was the one that took him up. Mr. Kennedy was the one that reported him, and they took him down there behind the cell-house and catted him. I stood out in the yard, and not only me but twenty or more counted. I counted forty-seven strokes of the cat. They hit him that much.

Q. By Mr. Patten: What kind of a cat is it?

A. Thirteen strings, made out of sole leather; altogether about three feet long; the strings about that thick [indicating with point of pen knife]. I counted forty-seven licks, and some other man says they hit him sixty-five, but I counted forty-seven, and left because I got nervous, hearing him hollering so and the terrible groans. You could hear the licks clear across the yard every time they hit him, and after they catted him they took him over to the shop and worked him that afternoon. He was taken over to the hospital the next morning. Friday he was licked and Saturday he went to the hospital to get excused.

Q. How long ago did this happen?

A. By being here so long it appears like things happened only yesterday that happened years ago; I think it has been 5 or 6 years ago.

Q. Who did the catting?

A. Captain Craig is the one who punished him; he used the cat himself; he done all the catting here.

Q. Was he excused on Saturday?

A. He was excused sometime during the day; he worked part of the day that day, and they took him over to the cell house sometime on Saturday. I was acting librarian then, and I came along by his cell Sunday morning, and Mungo told me he was sick, and I seen his eyes was all bloodshot. He asked if I wouldn't go and see the doctor for him; I told him I would. So I went down and told the guard that Mungo wanted to see him to go to the hospital. Then I went on to the hospital and saw Dr. Sherrod, and I told him that Mungo was up in the cell there sick, and his eyes were all bloodshot, and he wanted to see him. I don't know who went and got him, but anyhow they brought him up to the hospital, and he was entered, I think, from Sunday about 10 o'clock until, I believe, it was Monday morning; I won't be certain whether it was Monday or Tuesday. Arthur Bissett was acting as hospital steward then. We went over to his bed and took some sweet oil and rubbed his back with it. Arthur asked me if I would not help him. I told him yes; and I helped him there, put some on, and his back was just cut all to pieces. You never saw such a sight, gentlemen. The lashes went around under his stomach; the end of the lash stopped there, and from the end of the lash about an inch and a half it was turned blue.

Q. Was the flesh lacerated?

A. It was a perfect jelly, perfect blue mass, just like if you would mash blood blister. Around under the stomach here where these strokes struck, they were all black and blue, and it was turning purplish blue. That was on Sunday it commenced turning that way. I says to Arthur Bissett, the Steward: "Ain't there mortification setting in." Well, he looked at it, nodded his head, and " That's just what it is." We turned and rubbed it, that was late in the evening, and he kept at it all night. Mungo would jump and raise in his bed, with a wild look in his eyes. Of course, I was in bed. I did not go over to him, but the nurse would lay him back in the bed and ask what is the matter, and he would roll on his side and halloo: "Oh, my God, kill me, kill me, I am just dying with misery." The boys went over to him, told him not to make so much noise, remonstrated with him to keep as quiet as he could, so as not to disturb the other patients. Every once in a while, he would break out and jerk himself, spring up in bed, getting almost on his feet. The nurse would go and catch him,

and set him down in bed, The next morning just before
breakfast, Mungo came into the water-closet, and sat down
on the water-stool there, with his hands on his head in that
way [indicating], and I come along and said: "Mungo, how
do you feel this morning?" He just looked up at me and shook
his head a little. I caught hold of his hand. "Do you feel
like eating anything?", He said: "Oh, my God, Mack, don't
ask me." He went to raise his pants. I took hold of his pants
and helped him up. Arthur Bissett came in, and I believe a
man named Burnet. I said: "Boys, take hold of him," and
we took him to his bed. He said: "Don't lay me on my back,
for God's sake." He just turned over on the edge of his belly
and didn't lay half a minute till he sprung up and fell back
dead. By the strokes being on the spinal column on the seven
nerves connected with the heart on the back here. They extend over the heart back under the shoulder; by them being
bruised, and the blood bruised, mortification set in. Mortification is what killed him.

Q. Can you refer us to men who know about this matter?

A. Captain Harveston, and Rev. M. E. Boring. In regard
to O'Neil, you can send for Carnaham; he knows about his working in the shop. Mr. Lyons was the foreman, and Mr. Good-
man was the guard that reported him.

Q. What do you think was his trouble?

A. I don't know whether it was the bronchial tubes or
whether it was asthma, but that was my belief. From the
action of the man I think it was asthma, and the throat was
the cause of his trouble.

Q. What do you know of any rotten meat being brought
in here?

A. Rotten meat was brought in, and it had maggots—full-
grown skippers—and the man sitting right side of me, by the
name of Wilkerson, lives in Jennings County, was here for one
year for buying votes, a United States prisoner; he went out
and commenced vomiting, and the boys commenced speaking
about the meat, and knowing I was in the office a great deal—
I was then Librarian—spoke to me about the meat, and said:
"Don't you see it is rotten; don't you see the maggots? Why
in hell don't you tell the Warden?" I said, "Why don't you
tell him?" Well, the next day the meat was rotten again.
This time it was "salt horse"—corn beef. Captain Howard

was running a butcher shop then, him and George, and they would bring in the meat from this pork-house. When the boys seen this meat they stuck it under my nose again, and asked me if I had showed it to the Warden. I told them no, I did not. I brought a piece in here and showed it to Rev. M. E. Boring, Chaplain, and when I stuck it under his nose he reared back. He told me to take it in to the Warden. I went in to show it to the Warden; he was not around here any place. I spoke to Mr. Huette, the Clerk, but he would not look at it. He said it was none of his business; he had nothing to do with it at all. He says: "Mack, I can not do anything; I have nothing to say." That meat come right across from over there. Lynn and I both was right over there in the pork-house and seen them salt it; went there on purpose to see it. Captain Howard asked the prisoner over there that was butchering, "Did you salt that meat; you are certain you made a stiff brine of it?" He said "Yes, sir." It was already spoilt, and would slip when we lifted it out of the brine. When they were cooking the meat you could smell it all over the yard. I went to the cook and asked him, "Why in the d—l do you cook that meat; you know that meat is rotten?" He said, "Mack, they know it is rotten. I have orders to cook it, and you know I can't help myself. I will put it on the table if it stinks every man in the dining-room."

Q. How often did that occur?

A. Every time we had beef, pretty near. I showed some of this meat to Dr. Sherrod, and I says, "Doctor, you control the cooking of this meat." He said, "H— and d—, they pay no more attention to what I have to say than they do to you." I took this meat down and told Dr. Hunter about it, showed him the meat, and he jumped on the Warden about it. The Doctor told me the Warden told him the butcher imposed upon him. I told him he had been imposed upon for a good while—five or six years. Captain Howard promised Dr. Hunter it never should occur again.

Q. And then did it occur?

A. It did not occur very often after Dr. Hunter came in.

By Mr. Patten:

Q. State if Dr. Norvell interested himself in having the use of the cat abolished.

A. Well, I could not say. I never knowed a man talk to any of these Directors and get anything out of them.

Q. How long is it since they catted anybody?

Q. Not since three years ago, the 27th of October, the last 1 know of.

Q. Has the treatment of men been any better?

A. Before Dr. Hunter came it was terrible, since then it has been better.

Q. Dr. Hunter and Dr. Norvell were elected at the same time.

A. Yes, sir; Dr. Norvell, when he first started in, for the first year and a half, everything went on all right, but after Captain Howard was re-elected, you might as well talk to a post. There haven't been any Directors here for the last two years.

William Christenberry having been duly sworn, testified as follows:

Q. By Mr. Alexander: How long have you been here?

A. Fifteen years.

Q. How long did you come for?

A. For life; for murder.

Q. From what county?

A. Owen.

Q. Did you know a man in the Prison named O'Neil?

A. Yes, sir.

Q. What do you know, if anything, about this man O'Neil having been punished here at any time?

A. I know he was punished. I was working at the hospital at the time he was brought up there. Six years ago this month, a man came there and reported there was a man found dead at the door. The doctor told him he could not bring a dead man back to life. They brought him up there. He was dead when they brought him. His arms were stiff and stayed up, and then when you press them down to his body, they would fly up in the same position [indicating].

Q. What did you help do with the body, if anything?

A. I helped wash it and dress it for burial.

Q. Was McDonald Cheek there at the time?

A. I think he was working in the hospital.

Q. Dr. McClure, was he there?

A. Dr. Jesse McClure was there ; yes, sir. Dr. Sherrod was head physician.

Q. What did you hear Dr. Sherrod say about this man ?

A. They pronounced it heart disease, and after they went away the doctor said there was no more heart disease about that man than there was about him.

Q. Who was it pronounced it heart disease ?

A. Jesse McClure and the coroner, Jacob Ross. They went there and kind of made an investigation.

Q. Did the Coroner examine any witnesses?

A. Some few of the guards.

Q. Do you know what this man was punished for ?

A. For not being able to do his work.

Q. What about his being sick ?

A. He was sick, and the doctor had excused him and sent him to the cell-house sick, and they took and chained him up in the cell unbeknownst to Dr. Sherrod, who had excused him and sent him to the cell-house as a sick man not able for duty.

Q. You say the Coroner pretended to make an investigation, and Dr. McClure said it was heart disease ?

A. Yes, sir.

Q. What do you know of one of these guards, Hilliard, and Dr. Sherrod having a quarrel about it?

A. I heard such as that, but could not say whether they did or not.

Q. Where did they keep this dead man, in the dead-house, until they buried him ?

A. Yes, sir, after they brought him from the cell. The Legislative Committee was here the very morning they brought him down. They seen him—a portion of them; not all.

Q. Did they cut him open and examine him ?

A. Yes, sir.

Q. Did they take his heart and lungs out?

A. I could not tell ; I was not there. I seen his heart there when I went to dress him for burial. His hands would not stay down on his body so as to keep them down.

Q. How long after he died was it that he was buried ?

A. They kept him there one night, and I ain't sure but two.

Q. Was there anything said about being in a hurry and getting him dressed and getting the shroud?

A. No, sir, nothing said of it that I heard.

Q. Do you know how long this man was up there in this cage?

A. No, sir, I ain't positive. It was about seven or eight days from the time the doctor excused him that they brought him down dead. Whether he was in the cage all that time I could not say.

Q. Did you ever hear Captain Howard say anything about it?

A. I never heard Captain Howard open his mouth about it.

Q. Did you know a man named Mungo?

A. Yes, sir.

Q. And about his being catted. Do you know the number of strokes?

A. No, sir, I did not count the strokes, but the catting must have continued ten or fifteen minutes, if not longer.

Q. Did you see him after he was catted?

A. Not for some time afterward.

Q. How long after?

A. It was, I suppose, a week or ten days.

Q. Did you see his body?

A. No, sir, I did not see the body. I did not see him after he was dead.

Q. When you did see him, what seemed to be his condition?

A. He said they had ruined him catting him. Said they had broken something inside of him. He never showed me any marks.

Q. What about any other persons being catted?

A. That was a frequent case.

Q. How long is it since anybody was catted?

A. Four years and over, as I understand.

Q. What kind of a cat is it?

A. Heavy blacksnake stock, from nine to ten cat-tails.

Q. Did they give it to you?

A. Yes, once.

Q. How was it done?

A. You are perfectly naked, with the exception of your pants, and get down on your hands and knees. John Craig did the catting. The man that whips stands behind.

Q. How many licks did they give you?

A. Seven.

Q. Did it cut the skin?

A. Opened it like a knife every time I was struck. It was sore for two weeks. Never put anything on it except a little liniment oil I got myself.

Q. What were you punished for?

A. I was at work in the foundry at the time. The contractors gave me permission to go into the carpenter shop for kindling wood to build a fire in the cupola, and a man by the name of Isgregg was foreman of the shop, and he told me that hereafter I would always find my kindling wood at that end of the bench; so I went there to get the wood, and he reported me for getting wood without permission. We got into some words about it. I said, "Mr. Isgregg, if I was a free man you wouldn't talk that way. Mr. Perin told me I could have the kindling wood, and you told me where I would always find it." He went and reported me for "sass." Craig would not listen to me at all, but took me behind the cell-house and gave me the seven licks. The knots in the end of them are like shot. They sunk into the flesh just like a bullet.

Frank Myers, having been duly sworn, testified as follows:

Q. By Mr. Patten: How long have you been here?

A. About ten years and seven months.

Q. You were out awhile on parole?

A. Yes, sir; I was out not quite eleven months.

Q. Was you here at the time the rumor was in circulation about a man by the name of Goddard that was cruelly punished, and reported that he was burnt in the furnace?

A. I don't remember anything of the circumstances.

Q. What department was you in?

A. I worked in several departments here in my time.

Q. You have been here all of the time Howard was Warden?

A. No, sir. I am not certain when he came here. I came in 1875, in October, and my recollection is he came in June following.

Q. Well, since he was Warden, do you remember about that circumstance?

A. I don't remember anything of that kind, sir.

Q. How does it happen that you did not hear the report?

A. I could not tell you. I never heard of a man being burnt here in my time.

Q. Did you know of the death of Goddard?

A. I don't know the man at all. No, sir; I don't recollect the name of Goddard. I recollect a man by the name of Godfrey, but Godfrey went out here.

Q. Have you any recollection of a man named O'Neil, who was here?

A. I have heard that name.

Q. Do you know anything of his death.

A. No, sir; I understood he died in the cell. Heard that rumor. That is all I know about it.

Q. Did you know of a convict of the name of Mungo, who died here; was catted five or six years ago.

A. No, sir.

Q. Did you ever see any man catted, or hear him catted?

A. I never saw a man catted. I believe I did hear it once, walking on the outside of the cell-house. It sounded like something of that kind.

Q. Was it usual to cat men?

A. They used to cat men here.

Q. Did they ever punish you that way?

A. No, sir.

Q. Was you in and about the office much?

A. I worked about the office four months at one time.

Q. Was you a trusty?

A. Yes, sir, part of the time.

Q. In what department did you work?

A. I worked at Captain Howard's house awhile, and then I worked at the barn.

Q. You were on good terms with Captain Howard?

A. I don't know on what kind of terms I was.

Q. How did he treat you?

A. He treated me all right.

Q. Was you ever punished?

A. No, sir, I can't say I was punished. I was turned in from the outside.

Q. What for?

A. I could not tell you what that was for. One time I was turned in for disobeying his rules; the other time I don't know what for.

Q. You don't know anything in reference to these men we have asked you about?

A. Not a thing, sir.

Q. How long are you sentenced for?

A. Twenty-one years.

Q. What for?

A. Manslaughter.

Q. You are the man Governor Gray sent back after being paroled?

A. Yes, sir.

Q. Have you anything to state before the committee?

A. I have no grievances to make.

George Bachtel, having been first duly sworn, testified as follows :

Q. By Mr. Patten : How long have you been here?

A. Almost twelve years.

Q. How long were you sent for?

A. For life, charged with murder.

Q. Do you recollect anything about a man named O'Neil?

A. Yes, sir. I was cook in the Hospital in '80 and remained there until March, 1881.

Q. Do you remember when O'Neil died.

A. Yes. O'Neil was brought up in February, 1881. He was brought up to the Hospital one night about 12 o'clock. He was sick. In the morning he made his appearance before the Doctor and said he was sick. The Doctor told him there was not a d— thing the matter with him, and told him to go to his shop. The man said he was not able to go to his shop, and a man by the name of Jack Hilliard, guard there, said, " Turn him over to me ; I will make him work." He was turned over to this man. He was taken to the cage, I suppose, for three days and nights. He was brought back dead.

Q. Did you see him after he was dead?

A. I did.

Q. State what condition he was in.

A. I could not tell whether he was a white man or a nigger when he was lying in bed—he was so dirty.

Q. What position?

A. I saw him in the dead-room, and he was lying with his hands over his head, with hands locked over his head. His eyes was glaring. I said the man was not dead. He was stiff and had his hands set there, perfectly tight. When they washed his hands, they placed them across his breast and tied a string around his body to hold his hand—keep them from flying back.

Q. Did you see any post-mortem examination?

A. There were three doctors down, I believe from Jeffersonville. I don't know as I could give their names. They held a post-mortem over him. Took his inwards out, his heart, lungs and liver; took them out and examined them. They gave some decision before the Committee. The House Committee was here that day.

Q. Was you present when the House Committee was there?

A. Yes, they held a kind of inquest in the hospital ward, and the young Dr. McClure, Steward, was there, and he took his heart and opened it. I stayed by when he examined it. A man by the name of McDonald Cheek helped him do that. There were a few drops of clotted blood in the bottom of the heart. I believe the young doctor said the heart had a little more fat on than usual. He said he had a perfect set of lungs and a good liver. He did not give any decision about him as to what was the cause of his death.

Q. What was the general rumor as to that?

A. The general rumor all over the prison was that the man died in the cage.

Senator Rahm, having been duly sworn, testified that he never had any business transaction with Director Norvell, or any other of the Directors of the Prison, and that no telegram had ever been sent by him to any of the Directors, nor had he ever received any such from said Directors, and that all statements made to the contrary were false, and that he was not connected either directly or indirectly with the election of A. J. Howard as Warden.

155

EXHIBIT " A."

[No. 1.]

JEFFERSONVILLE, IND., May 29, 1879.

No...........

FIRST NATIONAL BANK,

OF JEFFERSONVILLE,

Pay to A. J. Howard, Warden, or order, six thousand dollars.
$6,000.   I. B. MERIWETHER.

[Indorsed as follows:]

A. J. HOWARD, *Warden.*

Pay W. H. Fogg, cashier, or order, for collection for Citizens'
National Bank, Jeffersonville, Ind.

JOHN ADAMS, *Cashier.*

[No. 2.]

JEFFERSONVILLE, IND., Sept. 16, 1879.

{ 2-cent
  stamp. }   FIRST NATIONAL BANK,

OF JEFFERSONVILLE,

Pay to James G. Harrison (costs, etc.,) or order, one hundred
and twenty-nine dollars. $129.

I. B. MERIWETHER.

[Indorsed as follows:]

JAMES G. HARRISON.

Credit accepted.

FIRST NATIONAL BANK, NEW ALBANY, IND.,

WM. N. MAHON, *Cashier.*

[No. 2.] Costs in suits of N. W. Car Company at the suit of
the Warden of the Prison, wherein he claimed that certain fix-
tures erected by the company belonged to the State, because
being attached to the realty, and which was decided against
the Warden, and in which suit the Warden paid all the costs,
but not a part of the $6,000.

EXHIBIT "B."

BILLS PAYABLE.

M. V. McCann, coal	$1,642	45
Payne & Ragsdale, provisions	786	25
E. C. Eaken & Co., groceries	1,474	81
Lewman Bros., drugs and hardware	673	82
Jeffersonville Gas Company, gas	324	00
Perin & Gaff, merchandise	147	93
Sundry newspapers, labor advertisements	185	82
Geo. Willacy, queensware	30	80
O. F. Zimmerman, (?)	40	25
Myers & Bros., lumbermen	45	12
Chas. Nagle, ice	25	00
J. H. Zinsmeister & Bro., groceries	34	05
L. P. Byland, teamster	151	50
E. J. Howard, lumber	156	42
Ahrens & Ott, pumps, etc	74	30
Geo. H. Frank, saddlery	34	00
Geo. Hulzbog, carriage-maker	33	70
J. H. Hodapp, produce	178	65
P. Treacy, grocery	3	44
Oglesby & Dustin, produce	65	50
B. F. Babbitt, soap	38	99
Ohio Valley Telegraph Company, dispatches	8	90
G. W. Baxter, Deputy Warden	6	80
A. M. Bloom, meats	1,134	00
Salaries for November	2,229	82
Salaries for December	2,512	23
Salaries for January	2,528	47
Seymour Woolen Factory, balance	371	90
Total	$14,938	92
Seymour Woolen Factory	$1,025	33